■■■■■■■■■■■■■■■■■■■■■■■■■■■■■■■■■■■■■■■

Look for my first book on the charming and quaint Cotswolds:

**Garden Tours of England- The Cotswolds**

■■■■■■■■■■■■■■■■■■■■■■■■■■■■■■■■■■■■■■■

# GARDEN TOURS
# OF
# ENGLAND

## Self Guided Tours
## of the
## SOUTHERN REGION
Dorset, Hampshire, Kent, Surrey,
Sussex, Wiltshire

## Bonnie Randall

Photographs and Illustrations by
Greg Randall

Windsor Hill Publishing

Illustrations, Maps & Photographs: Greg Randall
Cover Design: Greg Randall & Bonnie Randall

Distributed U.S.A.: Windsor Hill Publishing


Randall, Bonnie, 1949-
Garden Tours of England- The Southern Region
1. Garden Tour- England, 2. Guidebooks, 3. Kent,
4. Surry, 5. Sussex

ISBN-0-9656510-1-0

Printed in the USA by

MORRIS PUBLISHING
3212 East Highway 30 • Kearney, NE 68847 • 1-800-650-7888

Cover Photo: Scotney Castle, Kent, England

■ ■ ■ ■ ■ ■ ■ ■ ■ ■ ■ ■ ■ ■ ■ ■ ■ ■ ■ ■ ■ ■ ■ ■ ■ ■ ■ ■ ■ ■ ■ ■ ■ ■ ■ ■ ■ ■ ■

To
MUMSIE
Who taught me about strength & courage
and who gives me lots of love.

■ ■ ■ ■ ■ ■ ■ ■ ■ ■ ■ ■ ■ ■ ■ ■ ■ ■ ■ ■ ■ ■ ■ ■ ■ ■ ■ ■ ■ ■ ■ ■ ■ ■ ■ ■ ■ ■

The charm of Tudor architecture
can be found all over the region.

# • TABLE OF CONTENTS •

Kent is well know for growing hops
and for drying them in **Oasthouses**.

# • INTRODUCTION •

My husband and I started visiting the wonderful gardens in England several years ago. In preparation for each trip we assembled our collection of picture books, guide books, garden books and the atlas and proceeded to map out our trip. We spent what seemed like days and, although it was a labor of love, it was a very complicated process.

The goal of this book is to take most of the confusion and complications out of your planning. It will provide you with the information and directions you will need to really enjoy your trip. Remember, unlike in the U.S., every garden is not open daily from 9:00 to 5:00. Infact, some gardens are only open one day a week and some are only open between 2:00 and 6:00 in the afternoon. Directional signs are, let's face it, different and not always terribly clear. Then there are those roundabouts and you have to drive on the left hand side of the road. Well, believe me it's all worth it and this book will make your trip a lot easier.

This second book is on the southern region of England and covers parts of five counties from Bath to the Dover coast. This is a much larger territory than the first book on the Cotswolds and much more diverse in climate, topography, architecture and garden style. You will find quaint villages, countryside dotted with sheep and cattle, hopfields, vineyards and perfect conditions for growing rhododendrons and azaleas. More importantly, you will find some of the most famous gardens in Europe and several other gardens that, although not nearly as famous, are just as wonderful.

This book describes 18 tours. They are organized by day of the week, with the intention that you will not have to drive far between gardens or feel the need to rush from one to the other. First, determine the day (or days) of the week that you have available. Then find the tours that are open on those days and finally, select the specific tour (s) you are interested in. Brief descriptions and histories of each garden are provided to help you make your selection. Under "List of Publications" you will find several suggestions for colorful picture books that focus on this region and there are many more to choose from in your local book stores. Purchase one or two and get a glimpse of the wondrous gardens that await you.

There are many kinds of gardens in these tours. Some are beautiful flower gardens with herbaceous borders and climbing roses. Some are very formal with large fountains and glorious sculptures and for some, the beauty is found in the history and architecture. For all of the gardens, the enjoyment is in the whole; the design, the history, the house (castle or manor), the countryside and the garden. Take time to experience it all!

It's time to get started, there's a lot to see and no time to waste!

# GARDEN TOURS
# OF
# ENGLAND

# THE
# SOUTHERN REGION

Dorset, Hampshire, Kent, Surrey,
Sussex, Wiltshire

# ENGLAND
## MAP

# SOUTHERN REGION
## MAP

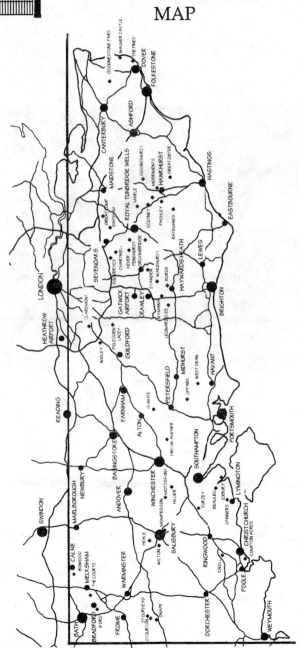

Cotswold stone walls reach into
the county of Wiltshire.

# • HELPFUL HINTS •

• The maps you will find in this book are useful. They are drawn to scale and you should have no trouble following them but, an atlas or road map of England is a must! There are numerous country roads and if you take a wrong turn, you can get confused and lost very quickly. Maps are available at book and travel stores and you should pick one up before you leave.

• Wear comfortable shoes. You will be doing a lot of walking and most of the time it's on dirt or gravel and up and down stairs.

• Wear comfortable clothes. In the summer you may be able to dress light but always bring along a sweater or sweatshirt and possibly a lightweight jacket. Warmer clothes will probably be needed in the spring and fall. A rain coat or slicker is good too.

• Make sure an umbrella is available all year round. We've been very lucky in all our trips but that doesn't mean you will be.

• Bring lots of film. Although there is film and disposable cameras everywhere, it's never around when you really want it and it's usually more expensive.

• Keep your eyes and ears open, many private homes open-up their gardens to the public one or two afternoons a year. If you are lucky, you might have the opportunity to visit a few. Look for signs along the road or in the towns and villages you are visiting. Also, *The Yellow Book* on the "List of Publications" can be ordered and will provide a lot more information on local gardens.

• This area is chock full of charming inns and B&B's; The Old Manor Hotel near Trowbridge, Wallett's Court Hotel near Dover, Wykeham Arms in Winchester, Sissinghurst Bed & Breakfast at Sissinghurst and Kennel Holt in Cranbrook are but a few. See "List of Publications" for further information or contact your travel agent.

Hints (continued):

• Many of the gardens have food services for lunch and / or tea. Usually nothing extravagant but frequently tasty (some of the pastries at tea are great). There is also hearty fare at most of the pubs and there are little restaurants in many towns and villages.

• I recommend you join the National Trust if you plan on visiting three or more National Trust gardens during your visit (two people, six total admissions). See page 8 for more information on the National Trust.

• The guide books and maps you find at many of the gardens are invaluable and are usually worth the few pounds. The National Trust books are especially good.

• Many of the gardens in this book are open on days other than those listed in the tours. See Garden Particulars on pages 129 thru 131 for further information.

• There are several gardens listed in Garden Particulars (pages 129 thru 131) and Garden Descriptions (pages 93 thru 105) that are not included in the tours. These are not quite up to my standards but that doesn't mean they aren't worth a visit if you are in the area.

• The months, days and times of operation were confirmed prior to publication of this book. Keep in mind that changes may be made to these schedules. It is advisable to confirm the times prior to setting out on your day's tour.

• There were so many interesting benches in the gardens we visited that we decided to start a picture collection. You will find several of these throughout this book. Hope you enjoy!

• We found so many new gardens or newly planted gardens in this region. It will take time for them to mature. I would love to hear your comments on how these gardens are progressing. Write to me at Windsor Hill Publishing, 119 Poppy Court, Walnut Creek, Ca. 94596

## Transportation

There are several types of transportation available. The simplest is to rent a car and drive yourself. You will be driving on the left side on very narrow roads but it won't take long to adjust. Mid sized cars are the best and ask for an automatic unless you are experienced with a stick. Autos can be rented at the airports and in many of the larger cities. Check with your travel agent or your favorite rental company for locations and availability before you leave on your trip. Remember, our maps are helpful but you really do need an atlas or a good road map of England.

You can also rent a car with driver. This is a relaxing way to travel especially if you just want to take a couple day trips. Although, in many cases, the cars are sedans not limos, they are very comfortable and you can just sit back and enjoy the countryside. If you are as lucky as we were on a couple of occasions, your driver will be a retired major or history professor with some wonderful stories about the towns and taverns you see. You can let your finger do the walking or you can ask at your hotel. This is a common practice and should be readily available even in some of the smaller towns.

Trains can be fun. If you are staying in London and want to spend a few days in the country, you can take a train to a central location such as Southampton or Royal Tunbridge Wells and rent a car or a car and driver there. The trains in Britain are great! They are clean, safe and on schedule. First class is worth the few extra pounds. Information on passes and schedules are available through your travel agent or the British Tourist Board.

If you are planning a trip to Paris, the Eurostar train through the Chunnel is a terrific way to go. We discovered that you don't have to go into London to catch the train. You can pick it up at Ashford, just a few miles west of Dover. Reservations are necessary. You can make arrangements through your travel agent before you leave on your trip or you can call (0345 30 30 30) anytime during your trip.

# THE NATIONAL TRUST

The National Trust, a registered charity, was set up in 1895 to promote "the permanent preservation, for the benefit of the nation, of lands and tenements (including buildings) of beauty or historic interest". The Trust currently cares for almost 600,000 acres of outstanding countryside, 555 miles of unspoiled coastline and has more than 300 historic houses and gardens open to the public.

The Trust is able to declare its property "inalienable" by an Act of Parliament in 1907. This means that once land and buildings are in the Trust's ownership, they can never be sold or mortgaged (although they can be leased). Ownership by the Trust guarantees protection for generations to come.

Memberships in the National Trust provides 45% of the annual income needed by the Trust to look after its properties. Members are given free admission to houses and gardens in its care in recognition of the support members give the Trust.

Americans can also join The Royal Oak Foundation which is the U.S. membership affiliate of the National Trust. The Royal Oak foundation actively supports the Trust's mission and promotes cultural exchanges through scholarships and internships.

Your yearly membership allows free admission to all N.T. properties, a discount on some merchandise and a year of N.T. publications.

Ask about becoming a member at any National Trust garden or contact the Royal Oak Foundation at 285 West Broadway, Suite 400, New York, N.Y. 10013-2299, (212) 966-6565, fax (212) 966-6619.

The Courts

Sissinghurst Gardens

Nymans Gardens

# • THE SOUTHERN REGION •

The county of Kent is traditionally referred to as "the Garden of England" but this could apply to most of the southern region of England. The acid soils and mild climate of the southern coast are ideal for growing flowering shrubs such as rhododendrons, azaleas and camellias. The lushness and fertility of the southeast is perfect for roses, herbaceous plants, vineyards and hop fields. The diversity of plant life is dramatic and beautiful and can hardly be rivaled anywhere else in England.

This is also a region rich in a literary heritage that is unparalleled in England. Jane Austen (1775-1817) spent many wonderful years here and wrote six of her most famous novels. Charles Dickens moved to Kent in 1817 at the age of 5 and spent most of his childhood there. Many of his books dealt with locations in southeast England. Rudyard Kipling lived at Bateman's from 1902 to 1936 and Sir Arthur Conan Doyle was a frequent visitor to Groombridge Place. Alfred, Lord Tennyson (1809-1892), Virginia Woolf (1882-1941) and H.G. Wells (1866-1946) also spent a portion of their lives in this area.

Agatha Christie readers may find the town of Nether Wallop near Salisbury very familiar. It may be referred to by another name, St. Mary Mead, but it is still the home of Miss Marple.

A.A. Milne lived near Hartfield where he created his children's classic books featuring his son Christopher Robin and that 'silly old bear' Winnie-the-Pooh. In Hartfield you will find Pooh Corner where Christopher Robin bought his sweets and in Ashdown Forest you will find the landscape inhabited by Pooh and his friends.

You will find many centuries of history to explore from Canterbury Cathedral where Archbishop Thomas Beckett was murdered in 1170 to Hever Castle, the childhood home of Anne Boleyn. From the Norman stronghold at Leeds Castle that was once a palace for Henry VIII to Chartwell, the home Winston Churchill was forced to leave during World War II because it was too obvious a target for bombers.

On the eastern coast near Dover you can find remnants of the airfields that were home to the Royal Air Force who gallantly faced the enemy during those early years of World War II. Stand on the beach looking at those white cliffs and you can almost hear the roar of the engines.

The county of Kent is filled with garden centers as well as hop fields and vineyards. It's fun to wander through a few nurseries even if you can't bring any plants home. Remember, there's always seeds! You will frequently find a tea room in these garden centers. It is a place to refresh so you can keep on shopping. American nurseries might want to take a lead from this quaint custom.

One of the major ingredients in the making of beer is hops and you will find fields of hops everywhere in Kent. Look for the vines growing up long strings. Few of the rectangular shaped 'hoppehouses' (buildings for drying and packing hops) remain from the late 16th century. Round 'oasthouses' appeared in the 18th century but were then replaced once more by a rectangular type at the peak of the industry in the 19th century. Look for these buildings with the funny roofs, they're everywhere. Two good examples are at Sissinghurst and Great Dixter.

Beer making is big business but I was not aware that Kent had such a thriving wine industry. As we toured the region this past June enjoying the wonderful gardens, we discovered two very busy vineyards. The first, Lamberhurst Vineyard, was established in 1972 and is England's most famous vineyard. Winery tours and tastings are available. The second, Tenterden Vineyard, was established in 1977 and is one of England's leading wine producers. Winery tours and tastings are also available here.

We always take time to visit with the gardeners. They are usually quite friendly and happy to discuss their work. Two interesting topics came up in conversation during our last visit to this area, one was the distinct lack of well trained, experienced gardeners, the second, probably related in some ways, was the need to design gardens with more low-maintenance type plants. This most recent drought has also prompted many gardens to finally install some irrigation. It will be interesting to watch these changes over the next few years.

The Great Storm

It has been a number of years since the great storm of October, 1987 decimated thousands of acres of woodlands and toppled hundreds of ancient trees. It damaged several historic buildings and changed the character of many of the gardens all over the region. When you visit today it is hard to distinguish the changes that have taken place. But if you visited the gardens before the storm or have seen pictures, you know the changes are quite dramatic. We were visitors to Kent in the spring of 1988 when recovery was just beginning and there were many sad sights. Old, specimen trees and shrubs were destroyed and large sections of woodlands were completely flattened. There were encouraging sights too. Mature rhododendrons that had lost most of their branches were starting to leaf out from the remaining main trunk. Amazing!

Another smaller, but extremely destructive, storm occurred in 1990. Curiously, the American Redwoods proved to be more resistant than other species to the winds in both the storms of 1987 and 1990. The grounds at Bowood are a good example of their resilience.

Since 'the Great Storm' most gardens have recovered very nicely. In the case of Nymans, for instance, the lose of trees allowed more light into the garden and provided areas for new planting. I have tried to comment about the storms' affect on each garden. When you visit, try to picture how the landscape may have looked before the destruction.

A few of the towns and villages you may encounter in your travels are:

Bath has long been known as a health resort with mineral baths built by the Romans in the first century A.D. Extensive remains of these ancient baths were discovered between 1775 and 1881. There are many opportunities to enjoy a spa or you might just want to shop. A stroll through the residential areas provides a look at some very interesting architecture. The honey colored Bath stone fits beautifully with the Georgian style. Don't miss the Royal Crescent. You might even want to enquire about a hot-air balloon ride.

Bradford-on-Avon, a quaint little town not far from Bath and close enough to the Cotswolds to hold some of the same charm and characteristics such as Cotswold stone walls.

Royal Tunbridge Wells, in the middle of Kent, is a good central location for touring the gardens. There are restaurants and pubs to enjoy and many interesting shops to explore especially in the area in and around The Pantiles, a lovely colonnaded shopping street. The square clay paving stones or 'pantiles' you will find here were laid in the 18th century at the request of Princess Anne.

Winchester, once the joint capital with London and a bustling center of commerce, is still a very active and interesting town. One of the biggest attractions is the beautiful Winchester Cathedral. Here you will find 900 years of history including the place Jane Austen was buried.

I'm sure you all read *The Canterbury Tales* written by Geoffrey Chaucer in the late 14th century. You may want to make your own pilgrimage to this historic city and the Canterbury Cathedral, where Thomas Beckett was murdered in 1170. The cathedral has been the seat of the primate of the Church of England since 601. Although the city was hit by several bomb attacks in 1942, it retains its medieval character.

The prosperous little town of Petersfield is a good place to stop for lunch. But the best reason to stop is to visit the very English 'Bear Museum' (38 Dragon St.). The proprietor began her collection in 1981 and would be very happy to chat about her unique assortment of bears. There are also several new bears for sale.

Market Day has been held in Salisbury's town center on Tuesday and Saturday for 600 years. If you are in town on Market Day, stop by and get a feel for shopping in days of old. Salisbury Cathedral was built from 1220-1258 in the English Gothic style. Spend a little time here as a part of your visit to Mompesson House.

Bosham, along the southern coast of Sussex, was an important port in Anglo-Saxon times and remains a charming spot to visit today.

Along the eastern coast you can visit the towns of Sandwich, Deal and St. Margarets at Cliffe and you might even try to arrange a tee time at the historic golf course at Royal St. George.

Dover is a very busy port city with ships and ferries loading and unloading all along the harbor. You will find some good restaurants and shops for tee shirts and other souvenirs and the true 'white cliffs' of Dover.

Folkstone was developed as a seaside resort with the arrival of the railway from London in 1843-4. It is known for its cliff-top gardens and remains a major cross-Channel port.

A few other towns you might enjoy are Westerham near Chartwell, Burwash near Pashley Manor and Lyndhurst, not far from Exbury.

Mottisfont Abbey Gardens

# TOURS
# OF THE
# SOUTHERN REGION

Dorset, Hampshire, Kent, Surrey,
Sussex, Wiltshire

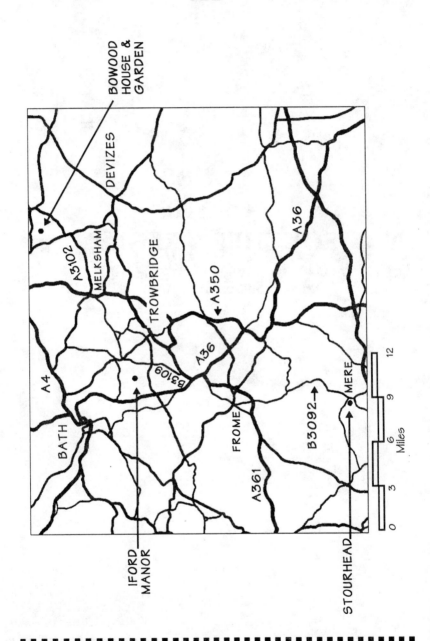

# TOUR #1

### * STOURHEAD
### * IFORD MANOR
### * BOWOOD HOUSE & GARDEN

## • DAILY EXCEPT MONDAY & FRIDAY •

In this tour you will find two of the finest landscapes of the 18th century. At Bowood, designed by 'Capability' Brown, there are also lovely formal terraced gardens and a fabulous fountain. At Stourhead you will not only enjoy an unbelievable collection of mature trees and shrubs but several magnificent follies. An enchanted and romantic terraced garden designed by Harold Peto awaits you at Iford Manor. Up to two hours are needed for Bowood and Iford and plan on two to three hours at Stourhead. Travel time between Bowood and Iford is 50 minutes. Travel time between Iford and Stourhead is 50 minutes.

### IFORD MANOR
- Hours of Admission: 2:00 to 5:00
- Location: 7 miles southwest of Bath on A36
  - If you cross the River Frome by way of the 13th century Iford Bridge you will find this enchanted and romantic garden designed by Harold Peto who made his home here from 1899 to 1933.
  - The first house was built in the late 15th century but it refurbished in the 18th Century to the Tudor style you see today.
  - Peto loved the time he had spent in Italy and he developed an extensive collection of statues and pots that you will find throughout this wonderful Italian-style terraced garden.
  - From the arched loggia immediately behind the house you can see Cotswold stone walls and terra cotta pots filled with flowers decorating steps that lead you up to two lovely terraces.
  - The first terraced area has a Mediterranean feel with tall Italian cypress, sun loving plants and a stone garden house.
  - The magnificent broad top terrace displays fine old stone columns and balustrades from Peto's collection, an octagonal summerhouse, borders with climbing wisteria and colorful peonies and an oval lily pond.
  - Note: Take your time, there is much to see. A must for anyone interested in garden design.

## STOURHEAD (N.T.)

- Hours of Admission: 8:00 to 7:00
- Location: at Stourton off B3092, 3 miles northwest of Mere
- One of the finest landscape gardens of the 18th Century. It was laid out between 1741 and 1780 by Henry Hoare. No famous name is attached to the design but it does show the influence of William Kent.
- The Palladian revival house was built between 1721 and 1725.
- Sir Richard Colt Hoare introduced flowering shrubs, in particular the rhododendrons, after he acquired the property in 1785.
- If you follow the high path it will take you through an extensive collection of trees that have matured into an unbelievable landscape. There are unusual and exotic trees and shrubs such as a huge monkey puzzle tree, a 150 year old tulip tree, maples, beeches, conifers and many more.
- Walk down to the path that encircles the lake. The path leads you through a wonderful woodland setting of rhododendrons, magnolias and colorful trees and provides vantage points to view several magnificent follies. Color is gorgeous in spring and vibrant in autumn.
- See if you can discover the elegant Pantheon built in 1753 that commands attention from every vantage point; the Temple of Apollo built in 1765; the Temple of Flora built in 1744; the marvelous stone Palladian Bridge; the Bristol High Cross from the 15th century; King Alfred's Tower built in 1772 and an obelisk built in 1839-40.
- If you want to see a fabulous grotto, Stourhead is the place. Constructed in 1748, you can actually walk in and explore. It is lined with limestone and there is a "porthole" that looks out onto the lake.
- The walled garden was built in the early 19th century to supply cut flowers and fruits & vegetables for the household.
- Note: Spread Eagle Inn, an old English pub near the entrance to the garden, is a great place for lunch or just a mug of beer. There are also 5 overnight rooms with bath.

Enjoy the elegant Pantheon from several vantage points at Stourhead.

The fabulous fountain
at Bowood House.

## BOWOOD HOUSE and RHODODENDRON WALK

- Hours of Admission: 11:00 to 6:00
- Location: 1 mile west of Caine on A4
  - One of the finest surviving landscapes by "Capability" Brown who began his work in 1763. There is over 2000 acres with a lake created by damning the Rivers Whetham and Washway.
  - The house was begun in 1720 and completed shortly after the 1st Earl of Shelburne purchased it in 1754. The Earl constructed the walled kitchen garden and a portion of the ha-ha.
  - The grounds around the house are a series of formal terraces. Columnar clipped yews rise out of areas of lawn and hundreds of roses bloom in neat beds.
  - One of the loveliest features is a fountain with stone steps climbing up either side and a lounging nude at the top. Look for the wonderful lions protecting the fountain. What expressions!
  - A newly planted partierre in front of the house is well done and very colorful but it will take a few years to realize its true beauty.
  - From the east terrace there is a breathtaking view of the pleasure grounds and 40 acre lake. A Doric Temple is in a striking position at one end of the lake.
  - A separate 50 acre rhododendron garden, open for six weeks in May and June, is a blaze of color.
  - As you walk through the woods you can hear the roar of the fabulous multi-tiered water cascade long before it is visible.
  - The storm of 1990 swept through and destroyed over 700 mature trees but many wonderful trees still stand including giant redwoods and 200 year old cypress.
  - Notes: You will find the laboratory where Joseph Priestly discovered oxygen gas in 1774. There are picnic grounds, a children's play area and a small garden center. Bowood Country Club is nearby for those "non-garden" people.

**OTHER GARDENS IN THE AREA**: THE COURTS, STOURTON HOUSE, SNAPE COTTAGE

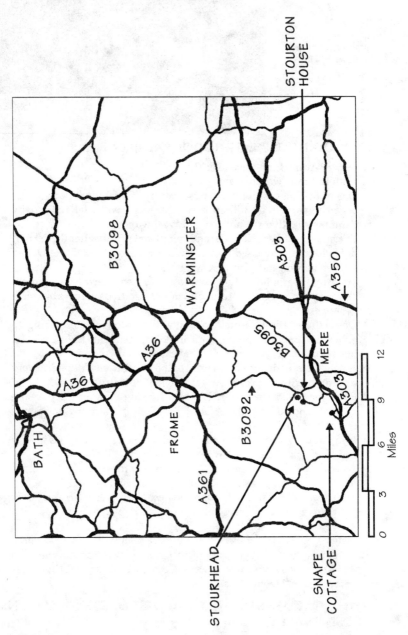

# TOUR #2

## * STOURHEAD
## * STOURTON HOUSE
## * SNAPE COTTAGE

## • SUNDAY, WEDNESDAY, THURSDAY •

These three gardens are a stone's throw from each other so there is plenty of time to enjoy. Stourhead is a fabulous landscape with a beautiful lake and several magnificent follies. Two to three hours are needed here. You might want to stop at the Spread Eagle Inn for refreshments before walking across the street to Stourton House, a charming and colorful cottage garden. Many flowers from the garden are collected, dried and offered for sale in beautiful bouquets. Just down the road is Snape Cottage, a small but lovely plantsman's garden. One to two hours are need for Stourton and Snape. Travel time between Stourhead and Stourton House is 5 minutes. Travel time between Stourton and Snape is about 10 minutes.

### SNAPE COTTAGE

- Hours of Admission: 2:00 to 5:00
- Location: southwest of Mere on A303
  - This is a lovely half acre plantsman's garden created since 1987. It was planted for year round interest with a special emphasis on old fashioned cottage garden perennials and plant history.
  - The pond was dug in 1989 and is filled with British native wild flowers.
  - You will find lovely views over the Blackmore Vale.
  - Take a few minutes to chat with Angela Whinfield, the lady of the house and creator of the garden.
  - Note: This is also a B&B. You will find it in the Garden Lovers Bed & Breakfast listed in the back of this book.

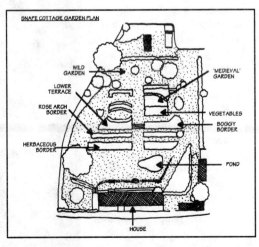

## STOURHEAD (N.T.)

- Hours of Admission: 8:00 to 7:00
- Location: at Stourton off B3092, 3 miles northwest of Mere
  - One of the finest landscape gardens of the 18th Century. It was laid out between 1741 and 1780 by Henry Hoare. No famous name is attached to the design but it does show the influence of William Kent.
- The Palladian revival house was built between 1721 and 1725.
- Sir Richard Colt Hoare introduced flowering shrubs, in particular the rhododendrons, after he acquired the property in 1785.
- If you follow the high path it will take you through an extensive collection of trees that have matured into an unbelievable landscape. There are unusual and exotic trees and shrubs such as a huge monkey puzzle tree, a 150 year old tulip tree, maples, beeches, conifers and many more.
- Walk down to the path that encircles the lake. The path leads you through a wonderful woodland setting of rhododendrons, magnolias and colorful trees and provides vantage points to view several magnificent follies. Color is gorgeous in spring and vibrant in autumn.
- See if you can discover the elegant Pantheon built in 1753 that commands attention from every vantage point, the Temple of Apollo built in 1765, the Temple of Flora built in 1744, the marvelous stone Palladian Bridge, the Bristol High Cross from the 15th century, King Alfred's Tower built in 1772 and an obelisk built in 1839-40.
- If you want to see a fabulous grotto, Stourhead is the place. Constructed in 1748, you can actually walk in and explore. It is lined with limestone and there is a "porthole" that looks out onto the lake.

- The walled garden was built in the early 19th century to supply cut flowers and fruits & vegetables for the household.
- Note: Spread Eagle Inn, an old English pub near the entrance to the garden, is a great place for lunch or just a mug of beer. There are also 5 overnight rooms with bath.

The Temple of Apollo
at Stourhead.

The impressive hedge of Leyland cypress at Stourton House.

## STOURTON HOUSE

- Hours of Admission: 11:00 to 6:00
- Location: 3 miles north of Mere next to Stourhead at A303
  - When you arrive at this English cottage garden, a charming woman will be there to greet you. Elizabeth Bullivant, the current owner, will be glad to chat with you about the garden or sell you a few of her own dried flowers.
  - The house was built in 1820 but Anthony & Elizabeth Bullivant bought the property in 1957 and began creating the garden. The garden was a mass of weeds and brambles but Elizabeth was drawn to the blue hydrangeas flowering in all the chaos; these same blue hydrangeas started the dried flower business.
  - Four acres of gardens have developed over several years. New garden areas have been created out of disasters such as trees blowing over in storms or rhododendrons dying in a drought.
  - A switchback hedge of Leyland cypress has taken 27 years to reach its impressive height and is clipped and shaped into an unusual wall. You will find nothing finer at Hidcote.
  - A pathway of delphiniums, a pergola covered with roses and wisteria, tree peonies and borders filled with beautiful herbaceous plants provide a riot of color from spring through fall.
  - You will also find a woodland garden filled with magnolias, rhododendrons, camellias and hydrangeas.
  - Topiaries, stone urns filled with flowers and a sculpture of a corseted lady diving into the lily pond add to the charm.
  - Elizabeth has experimented with drying many plants and finds that almost everything in the garden can be preserved.
  - Note: This is the family home so you may see a big, black lab, several small children or Mr. Bullivant (a real charmer) while wandering in the garden.

OTHER GARDENS IN THE AREA: IFORD MANOR, BOWOOD GARDEN, THE COURTS

# TOUR #3
## MAP

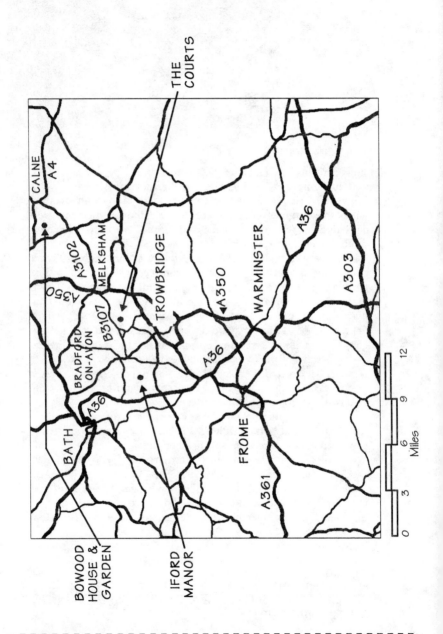

26

# TOUR #3

### * THE COURTS
### * IFORD MANOR
### * BOWOOD HOUSE & GARDEN

## • SUNDAY, TUESDAY THROUGH THURSDAY •

At his own home, Iford Garden, Harold Peto designed a romantic terraced garden and filled it with his terrific collection of Italian statues and pottery. The 20th century garden at The Courts is laid out in a series of rooms. You will find several lovely features here including 'dancing bear' topiaries. A colorful partierre and magnificent fountain in the terraced garden at Bowwod House are surrounded by a fine 'Capability' Brown landscape. One to two hours are need at each garden. Travel time between Iford and The Courts is 25 minutes. Travel time between The Courts and Bowood is 40 minutes.

### IFORD MANOR

- Hours of Admission: 2:00 to 5:00
- Location: 7 miles southwest of Bath on A36
  - If you cross the River Frome by way of the 13th century Iford Bridge you will find this enchanted and romantic garden designed by Harold Peto who made his home here from 1899 to 1933.
  - The first house was built in the late 15th century but it refurbished in the 18th Century to the Tudor style you see today.
  - Peto loved the time he had spent in Italy and he developed an extensive collection of statues and pots that you will find throughout this wonderful Italian-style terraced garden.
  - From the arched loggia immediately behind the house you can see Cotswold stone walls and terra cotta pots filled with flowers decorating steps that lead you up to two lovely terraces.
  - The first terraced area has a Mediterranean feel with tall Italian cypress, sun loving plants and a stone garden house.
  - The magnificent broad top terrace displays fine old stone columns and balustrades from Peto's collection, an octagonal summerhouse, borders with climbing wisteria and colorful peonies and an oval lily pond.
  - Note: Take your time, there is much to see. A must for anyone interested in garden design.

Enjoy a quiet moment in the garden house at The Courts.

## THE COURTS (N.T.)

- Hours of Admission: 2:00 to 5:00
- Location: 2.5 miles east of Bradford-on-Avon, south side of B3107 in centre of Holt
- Enclosed garden in the middle of a village, it looks inward with no views of the world around.
- An 18th Century stone house built by a cloth weaver who used the plentiful supply of water available for a cloth mill. The grounds have several relics of its cloth weaving past.
- Sir George Hastings occupied house from 1900-1911 and began the garden by planting yew hedges as background for his collection of stone statuary.
- In 1920 Major T.C.E. Goff and his wife moved in. Influenced by Gertrude Jekyll and Lawrence Johnston, Lady Goff created a seven acre garden laid out in a series of "garden rooms" to create a sense of surprise and mystery.
- The pillar garden with the central area of the lawn is dominated by eight stone pillars draped with "Iceberg" roses.
- Blue & yellow borders that surround the silver-leafed pears and other silver-gray foliage plants are at their best in the summer months with deep blue geraniums, various shades of blue and purple asters and the yellow of achilleas and *thalictrum*.
- Wonderful yew hedges include some bumpy topiaries that are suppose to represent funny, dancing bears.
- Lady Goff created the long rectangular lily pond has richly colored plantings on both sides including mixed colors of lilies.
- A pair of Venetian wrought iron gates separate the formal gardens from the 3.5 acre arboretum.
- Note: Some of my favorite features are the verandah porch, glass garden house and of course the dancing bears. Actually, this garden reminds me a little of my own.

## BOWOOD HOUSE and RHODODENDRON WALK

- Hours of Admission: 11:00 to 6:00
- Location: 1 mile west of Caine on A4
  - One of the finest surviving landscapes by "Capability" Brown who began his work in 1763. There is over 2000 acres with a lake created by damning the Rivers Whetham and Washway.
  - The house was begun in 1720 and completed shortly after the 1st Earl of Shelburne purchased it in 1754. The Earl constructed the walled kitchen garden and a portion of the ha-ha.
  - The grounds around the house are a series of formal terraces. Columnar clipped yews rise out of areas of lawn and hundreds of roses bloom in neat beds.
  - One of the loveliest features is a fountain with stone steps climbing up either side and a lounging nude at the top. Look for the wonderful lions protecting the fountain. What expressions!
  - A newly planted partierre in front of the house is well done and very colorful but it will take a few years to realize its true beauty.
  - From the east terrace there is a breathtaking view of the pleasure grounds and 40 acre lake. A Doric Temple is in a striking position at one end of the lake.
  - A separate 50 acre rhododendron garden, open for six weeks in May and June, is a blaze of color.

  - As you walk through the woods you can hear the roar of the fabulous multi-tiered water cascade long before it is visible.
  - The storm of 1990 swept through and destroyed over 700 mature trees but many wonderful trees still stand including giant redwoods and 200 year old cypress.
  - Notes: You will find the laboratory where Joseph Priestly discovered oxygen gas in 1774. There are picnic grounds, a children's play area and a small garden center. Bowood Country Club is nearby for those "non-garden" people.

Bowood House

**OTHER GARDENS IN THE AREA:** STOURHEAD, STOURTON HOUSE, SNAPE COTTAGE

# TOUR #4
## MAP

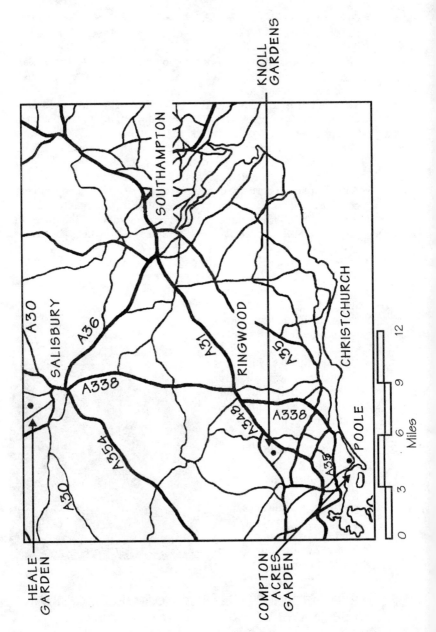

# TOUR #4

* KNOLL GARDENS
* COMPTON ACRES
* HEALE GARDENS

## • WEDNESDAY & THURSDAY •

A quintessential formal English garden, Heale Garden also contains an authentic 20th century Japanese garden with a bright scarlet bridge. Compton Acres and Knoll Garden are both 20th century gardens that may provide many good ideas for your own garden. One of the most enjoyable features at Compton Acres is the extraordinary Italianesque water garden with water lilies, roses and wonderful pieces of sculpture. Herbaceous borders, water falls and a magnificent dragon sculpture highlight the gardens at Knoll. At least two hours each are need to properly enjoy these gardens. Travel time between Heale and Knoll is 1.5 hours. Travel time between Knoll and Compton Acres is 35 minutes.

### COMPTON ACRES GARDENS
- Hours of Admission: 10:30 to 6:30
- Location: Canford Cliffs Road in Poole
  - This garden, on 15 acres of sloping land, was first created starting in 1914 by Thomas William Simpson. He designed a series of enclosed spaces linked by paths.
  - Neglected during World War II, the property was purchased in 1950 by J.S. Beard who restored the garden to its former glory.
  - The Japanese garden is completely authentic. It was built by a Japanese architect using ornaments and plants imported from Japan. The teahouse, heron sculptures and water fall are marvelous! There are lovely views down into the garden from several high points.
  - Tall hedges enclose the phenomenal Italianesque water garden. The central lake, covered with water lilies, is surrounded by thousands of roses, wonderful bronze and marble sculpture and stone urns.
  - In the extensive rock & water garden the water tumbles from the top banks down from pool to pool ending in a chain of lakes.
  - Note: Very popular for locals as well as tourists and can get a little crowded but well worth the effort. If you need ideas for your own garden this could be the place.

Compton Acres

## KNOLL GARDENS

- Hours of Admission: 10:00 to 5:30
- Location: off B3073 between Wimborne and Ferndown
  - A 20th century garden, the development of these 4 acres began just over 25 years ago.
  - See if you can spot all of the 5000 plants collected from all over the world. Don't worry, they are well labeled.
  - There is something for all seasons from carpets of bulbs and massed rhododendrons and azaleas in the spring to herbaceous & hardy perennials in the summer to the brilliant colors of autumn.
  - Enjoy the sights and sounds of the Water Garden. There are Cotswold stone walls, waterfalls and a wonderful display of large foliage plants surrounding two main pools filled with water lilies and big orange koi.
  - A great collection of alpine plants, nestled into large boulders on the side of a hill, form the Rock Garden.
  - In the Dragon Garden you will find a magnificent sculpture of a dragon surrounded by a partierre, the planting is seasonal, the design, formal. The sculpture is based on the legend of St. Dunston, the patron saint of goldsmiths and craftsmen whose emblem is a harp.
  - There are herbaceous borders, a penstemon walk, a large collection of hostas, wisteria climbing on a brick pergola and a friendly collie to greet you.
  - This well maintained garden continues to develop by experimenting with different plant combinations and extending the overall design.
  - Feel free to ask questions of any of the staff.
  - Note: Take a few minutes to browse through the garden center.

Fabulous
dragon sculpture
at Knoll Garden.

## HEALE GARDEN

- Hours of Admission: 10:00 to 5:00
- Location: 4 miles north of Salisbury on Woodford Valley Rd between A345 & A360
  - This handsome, rosy brick Carolean Manor House was originally built in the 16th century. It experienced many changes over the years including a devastating fire in 1835. After purchasing the house in 1894, Louis Greville restored and enlarged the house taking great care to match the original building.
  - King Charles II took refuge here during his escape in 1651 and remained for six nights.
  - A quintessential eight acre English garden on the River Avon with a formal layout, old brick walls, stone steps, old horse chestnuts and red beeches (two of my favorites) and a wonderful mix of plants.
  - In 1910 Harold Peto was hired to create designs for the garden. His chief work, the West Garden is a symmetrical terraced garden aligned on the front door. It was very formal and almost entirely herbaceous. The planting in this area was redone in the early 1960's using mixed shrubs, perennials and old roses.
  - The Japanese garden was originally created in the early 20th century by Louis Greville. After he spent some time in Tokyo in the diplomatic service, he became a devotee of Japanese culture. He brought back the tea house, the bright scarlet arched bridge, stone lantern and much more. The tea house with its interesting thatched roof provides an oriental setting for flowering cherries, magnolias and Japanese maples. The garden fell to disrepair during the war and was reclaimed starting in 1959 by the current owners.

Scarlet bridge at Heale.

  - Wonderful tunnels of espaliered apple trees divide the walled kitchen garden right down the middle.
  - An avenue of beech trees line the drive. Don't miss this while you are avoiding the sheep. They're everywhere!
  - Note: Two of my favorite little features are: the thatched roof dovecote (it really has doves) and the unique pyramid rose trellises. Arrive from the A345 side, it's a little shorter.

**OTHER GARDENS IN THE AREA:** WILTON HOUSE, MOMPESSON HOUSE, MOTTISFONT ABBEY, HILLIER GARDENS, SPINNERS, FURZEY GARDENS, EXBURY

# TOUR #5
## MAP

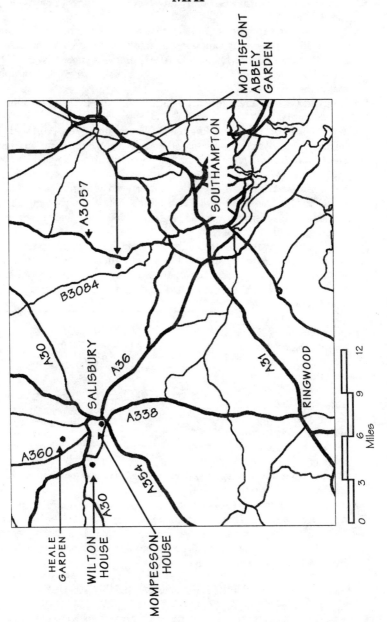

# TOUR #5
## * WILTON HOUSE
## * MOMPESSON HOUSE
## * MOTTISFONT ABBEY GARDEN

## • SATURDAY THROUGH WEDNESDAY •

Roses, roses, roses, that's what you will find at Mottisfont Abbey. The huge walled garden barely contains the internationally known collection of 350 varieties. When the roses are in bloom you will need at least three hours to properly inspect them all. Mompesson is a charming walled city garden with roses and colorful borders. Up to an hour is needed here. In sharp contrast, Wilton House is a lovely parkland with a stately Palladian Bridge and water garden connected by several bright red bridges. Up to two hours are needed at Wilton. Travel time between Mottisfont and Mompesson is 50 minutes. Travel time between Mompesson and Wilton is 20 minutes.

### MOMPESSON HOUSE (N.T.)

- Hours of Admission: 12:00 to 5:30
- Location: Cathedral Close, center of Salisbury

  - A small charming walled garden compliments the Queen Anne town house built in 1701 by Charles Mompesson.
  - The great wall of the Cathedral Close encloses one side of this intimate and traditional English garden.
  - You will find simple, herbaceous borders, a pergola covered with wisteria, honeysuckle and clematis and roses climbing on the brick walls and the house.
  - Much of garden has been replanted by the National Trust since 1975.
  - In the house look for the marvelous collection of 18th Century English drinking glasses and china figurines.
  - Note: Several rooms and the front of the house were used in the filming of Jane Austen's "Sense and Sensibility".

Brick walls enclose
the charming garden
at Mompesson House.

## MOTTISFONT ABBEY GARDEN (N.T.)

- Hours of Admission: 12:00 to 6:00
- Location: 4.5 miles northwest of Romsey
- William Lord Sandys converted this 13th century Augustinian priory to a house after the Dissolution. An elegant George II period brick house was grafted onto the remains of the 13th century abbey in the 1740's.
- A tributary of the River Test flows through the 21 acres of gardens and parkland creating a tranquil setting.
- The internationally known collection of roses are displayed within the brick walls of the old kitchen garden which dates from the 1740's. I had no idea the garden was this large, there are 350 varieties of roses from many parts of the world.
- Many of the roses were collected by Graham Stuart Thomas, who designed the garden in the 1970s.
- You will find a pergola covered with 'Adelaide d'Orleans' rose, interesting clipped topiaries, box hedged borders, mixed with apple trees and herbaceous plants and a ha-ha.
- Gilbert Russell was responsible for several of the garden's developments after he purchased the estate in 1934. Geoffrey Jellicoe designed the pleached lime walk in 1936 and the charming partierre was created by Norah Lindsay in 1938.

- The giant London plane tree near the house is really two trees that have combined to create the largest tree of its type in Britain. It probably dates from the first half of the 18th century.
- The National Trust acquired the property in 1957.
- There are many lovely features here but this is a 'rose' garden and the best time to visit is mid-June through July when the roses are at their height.
- Note: A wonderful place to stop for tea; served on blue and white Spode china in a charming tea room.

Roses, roses everywhere at
Mottisfont Abbey.

You will be impressed by the stately Palladian Bridge at Wilton House.

## WILTON HOUSE

- Hours of Admission: 11:00 to 6:00
- Location: 3 miles west of Salisbury on A30
  - The ancestral home of the Earl of Pembroke for 450 years. Henry VIII gave the property to Sir William Herbert in 1544. The Tudor Tower in the center of the east front is the only remaining portion of the original building to survive the fire of 1647. It was rebuilt in the Palladian style.
  - Within this 21 acres of parkland it is sad to say little of the 17th Century classical garden remains.
  - What you will find is a stately Palladian Bridge that provided the inspiration for bridges at Stowe and Prior Park, a lovely walled rose garden and a rose and wisteria covered pergola.
  - The water garden consists of three island planting beds that seem to float creating a moated effect. The islands are connected by several bright red oriental style bridges. Two of the beds are filled with roses and one with colorful perennials. Water lilies float on the water while irises and other unusual bog plants grow along the edges.
  - One of the more interesting details is the whispering bench. If you have a secret to tell, this is the place.
  - For the children there is a children's play area and Mary Hildesley's Wareham Bears, a collection of 200 miniature teddy bears (this is for children of all ages).
  - Note: The Double Club Room was the setting for the ballroom scene in the movie 'Sense *and Sensibility*'.

**OTHER GARDENS IN THE AREA:** HILLIER GARDENS, HINTON AMPNER, BROADLEAS GARDENS, HEALE GARDEN

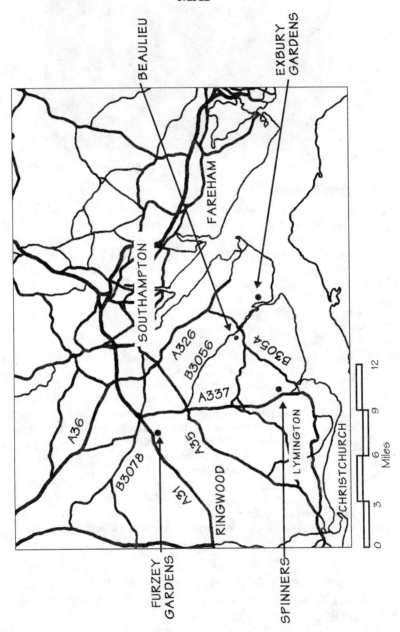

# TOUR #6

## * EXBURY GARDENS
## * FURZEY GARDENS
## * SPINNERS

## • DAILY EXCEPT SUNDAY & MONDAY •

Ideal climate and acid soils provide just the right conditions for the amazing spring gardens on this tour. First visit the world famous Rothschild garden at Exbury. The incredible color from over 1 million rhododendrons, azaleas and camellias will take your breath away. Three hours are needed to properly enjoy this garden. At Furzey Gardens you will also find many rare rhododendrons and azaleas and a wonderful collection of heaths and heathers. Spinners is a woodland garden rich in spring color and shade loving plants. One to two hours are needed at both Furzey and Spinners. Travel time between Exbury and Spinners is 35 minutes. Travel time between Spinners and Furzey is 40 minutes.

### SPINNERS

- Hours of Admission: 10:00 to 5:00
- Location: 2 miles north of Lymington off A337

  - Here you will find a plantsman's garden created by Mr. & Mrs. Peter Chappell over the past 25 years that has retained the spirit and atmosphere of adjacent New Forest
  - The woodland atmosphere is soothing and cool on a warm day. The path takes you through lush plantings of rhododendrons, azaleas and Japanese maples.
  - In spring the forest floor is rich with cyclamen, trilliums and hellebores while above there are magnolias, cream, apricot, scarlet and blue rhododendrons and many plants selected for their foliage and texture.
  - Several clearings provide massed beds of giant hostas and ferns colorful geraniums and brilliant irises and primulas.

The fabulous
collection
of rhododendrons
at Exbury is almost
overwhelming.

## EXBURY GARDENS

- Hours of Admission: 10:00 to 5:00
- Location: 2 miles south of Dibden Purlieu turn south off B3054
  - Lionel de Rothschild created this world famous 200 acre woodland garden starting in 1919. It remains in the Rothschild family today.
  - It took 150 men ten years to complete the garden.
  - There are over 1 million rhododendrons and azaleas in the Rothschild collection which is set in an informal parkland style. You will also see magnificent camellias, magnolias and hydrangeas.
  - The acid soil, mild temperatures and high humidity are ideal for growing these woodland plants.
  - Many of the plants were raised from seeds collected by plant hunters such as E. H. Wilson and Frank Kingdon-Ward on expeditions in the Himalayas and China.
  - Over 1000 new hybrids of rhododendrons and azaleas have been bred in the last 80 years.
  - The plants are spread over three areas: 1) Home Wood- where the earliest flowering shrubs stretch down to the river; 2) Witcher's Wood- named after local gypsy family; 3) Yard Wood- linked to the rest of the garden by a white bridge has a gnarled old yew tree reputed to have been recorded in the Domesday Survey. Did you know that yews provided bows for Norman & Plantagenet kings?
  - In late May you can enjoy the spectacular Lady Chamberlain's Walk which is lined with orange-salmon bell-flowered rhododendrons of that name.
  - There are miles of walks and thousands of trees and shrubs and you could easily spend an entire day.
  - Note: This place is incredible from late April through early June. There is so much color and beauty that you almost take it for granted. Remember to get a map or you could get lost.

## FURZEY GARDENS

- Hours of Admission: 10:00 to 5:00
- Location: 2 miles north of Lyndhurst on A337, turn west to Minstead
  - The eight acres of informal gardens was originally designed and planted in 1922.
  - Grassy paths wind through massed rhododendrons and azaleas.
  - Many of the rhododendrons & azaleas are rare and not seen elsewhere including one of the largest Himalayan rhododendrons I've ever seen.
  - You will also find a lovely collection of heaths and heathers that bloom all year round.
  - In the early spring there is a riot of color from the thousands of blooming crocus, bluebells and daffodils.
  - Many of the trees were chosen for their vibrant fall color (liquidamber, scarlet oak, witch hazel).
  - Much of the building materials used to build the 16th century cottage at the gardens entrance appear to have been first cut for ship building.
  - Look for the different materials used on the thatched roofs.
  - Note: This is a spring garden and a nice addition to your visit to Exbury.

Several types of thatched roofs are found at Furzey Gardens.

## OTHER GARDENS IN THE AREA: BEAULIEU, COMPTON ACRES, KNOLL GARDENS

# TOUR #7
## MAP

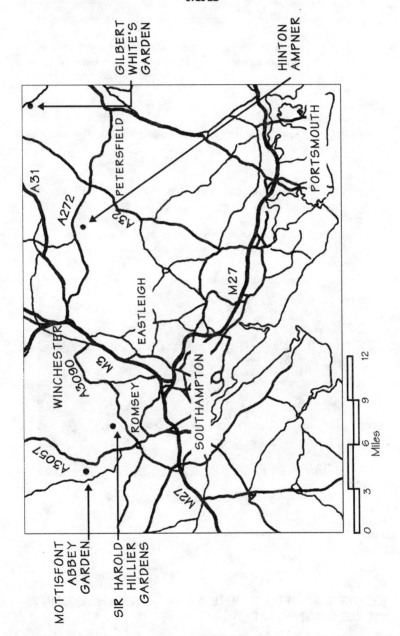

# TOUR #7

### * HINTON AMPNER
### * MOTTISFONT ABBEY GARDENS
### * GILBERT WHITE'S GARDEN
### * SIR HAROLD HILLIER GARDENS

## • SATURDAY, SUNDAY, TUESDAY, WEDNESDAY •

It's a busy day so no time to dawdle! Let's start at Hillier Garden, a 20th century arboretum and a great place for a picnic. Next stop is Mottisfont Abbey. If you love roses as I do, you will be delighted with this phenomenal collection of roses displayed within the old walled kitchen garden. In full bloom you will need up to three hours to really enjoy this garden. Set in the Hampshire countryside, Hinton Ampner is highlighted by a great collection of topiaries and a sunken garden. One to two hours are needed here. Last stop is Gilbert White's House, a quaint city garden. There are several lovely details and you will need about an hour. Travel time between Hillier and Mottisfont is 20 minutes. Travel time between Mottisfont and Hinton Ampner is 1 hour. Travel time between Hinton and G. White is 50 minutes.

## SIR HAROLD HILLIER GARDENS

- Hours of Admission: 10:30 to 6:00
- Location: 3 miles northeast of Romsey off A31
  - This 166 acre arboretum, founded in 1953, has one of the best 20th century collections of hardy trees and shrubs.
  - You will find 42,000 plants including the glorious colors of heathers, rhododendrons, azaleas and magnolias in the spring and vibrant colored oaks and maples in the fall.
  - Various plants are highlighted each month to help the visitor enjoy the experience. Late May, for instance, is a good time for "Johnson's Blue" geraniums, thalictrum, mountain laurel, flowering red horse chestnuts and several varieties of beech trees.
  - There are many special activities during the year that even casual visitors can participate in.
  - Note: Arboretums aren't for everyone put this one is really special. Besides, it's a good place to relax and have a picnic during your busy garden schedule.

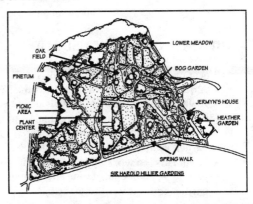

43

## HINTON AMPNER GARDEN (N.T.)

- Hours of Admission: 1:30 to 5:30
- Location: 1 mile west of Bramdean on A272
  - This Georgian house was built in the late 18th century. Although it has been changed several times over the years, it has retained its Georgian beauty. The property was in the Dutton family for nearly 400 years until it was bequeathed to the National Trust in 1985.
  - Set in Hampshire countryside, this garden was redesigned and extended in the 1940's and combines a formal design with lovely informal plantings.
  - Off the back of the house is a stone terrace with a great display of rock roses and other sun-loving, drought tolerant plants.
  - The Sunken Garden created in the 1930's provides a lovely display in spring and summer.
  - Two wonderful spinx adorn the stairway leading to the Lily Pond. Here you will find a long bed of "Iceberg" roses under planted with a deep pink diascia
  - If you happen to be there at the right time (mid to late June) there is a charming philadelphus walk, the fragrance is overwhelming.
  - One of the best collections of hedge and topiary clippings. Enjoy the big old mushroom topiaries on the terrace.
  - The area by the church comes alive in the early spring. Boxwood hedges and clipped yew cones enclose the beauty of flowering cherries, bluebells and daffodils.
  - After suffering greatly in the storms of 1987 & 1990, the gardens have undergone five years of restoration and are now flourishing.

Hinton Ampner

## GILBERT WHITE'S HOUSE AND GARDEN

- Hours of Admission: 11:00 to 5:00
- Location: in village of Selborne on B3006
  - A quaint city garden compliments the 18th Century house.
  - A walled garden with brick walls and yew hedges contain six planting beds filled with colorful perennials and roses.
  - You will also find a laburnum covered pergola, a topiary wall, a bog garden established in 1997 and an excellent example of a Ha-Ha.
  - Note: This is a work in progress but it is a good example of an urban garden. A great deal of time and money is being spent to restore this garden and it is worth the visit.

Mottisfont Abbey

## MOTTISFONT ABBEY GARDEN (N.T.)

- Hours of Admission: 12:00 to 6:00
- Location: 4.5 miles northwest of Romsey
- William Lord Sandys converted this 13th century Augustinian priory to a house after the Dissolution. An elegant George II period brick house was grafted onto the remains of the 13th century abbey in the 1740's.
- A tributary of the River Test flows through the 21 acres of gardens and parkland creating a tranquil setting.
- The internationally known collection of roses are displayed within the brick walls of the old kitchen garden which dates from the 1740's. I had no idea the garden was this large, there are 350 varieties of roses from many parts of the world.
- Many of the roses were collected by Graham Stuart Thomas, who designed the garden in the 1970s.
- You will find a pergola covered with 'Adelaide d'Orleans' rose, interesting clipped topiaries, box hedged borders, mixed with apple trees and herbaceous plants and a ha-ha.
- Gilbert Russell was responsible for several of the garden's developments after he purchased the estate in 1934. Geoffrey Jellicoe designed the pleached lime walk in 1936 and the charming partierre was created by Norah Lindsay in 1938.
- The giant London plane tree near the house is really two trees that have combined to create the largest tree of its type in Britain. It probably dates from the first half of the 18th century.
- The National Trust acquired the property in 1957.
- There are many lovely features here but this is a 'rose' garden and the best time to visit is mid-June through July when the roses are at their height.
- Note: A wonderful place to stop for tea, served on blue and white Spode china in a charming tea room.

**OTHER GARDENS IN THE AREA:** JANE AUSTEN'S HOUSE, GREATHAM MILL GARDEN

# TOUR #8
## MAP

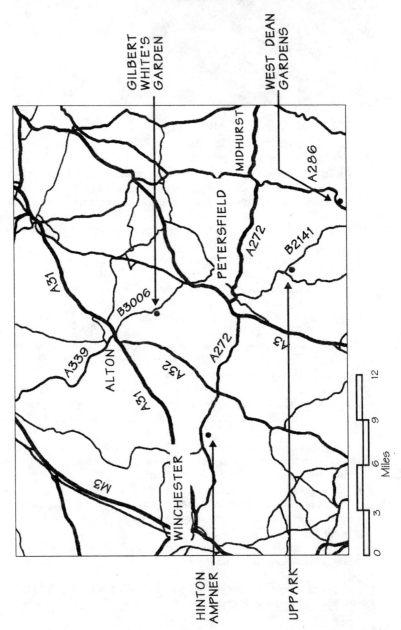

GILBERT WHITE'S GARDEN

WEST DEAN GARDENS

MIDHURST

PETERSFIELD

A286

A272

B2141

A31

B3006

A272

A339

A32

A3

ALTON

A31

M3

WINCHESTER

HINTON AMPNER

UPPARK

Miles

0    3    6    9    12

# TOUR #8

## * WEST DEAN GARDENS
## * GILBERT WHITE'S GARDEN
## * HINTON AMPNER
## * UPARK

## • SATURDAY, SUNDAY, TUESDAY, WEDNESDAY •

At West Dean, Harold Peto designed one of the most fabulous pergolas you will ever see. And this is only a part of this wonderful and relatively unknown garden. You will need two to three hours here. For a different look spend about an hour at Gilbert White's House, a charming city garden. At Hinton Ampner you will find a beautiful Georgian house and garden set in the Hampshire countryside. Enjoy the fragrance of the philadelphus walk and the discovery of several interesting topiaries. The gardens at Uppark may be simple but the views are extraordinary. One to two hours will be needed at Hinton and Uppark. Travel time between Gilbert White and West Dean is 1 hour. Travel time between West Dean and Uppark is 30 minutes. Travel time between Uppark and Hinton is 45 minutes.

## GILBERT WHITE'S HOUSE AND GARDEN

- Hours of Admission: 11:00 to 5:00
- Location: in village of Selborne on B3006
  - A quaint city garden compliments the 18th Century house.
  - A walled garden with brick walls and yew hedges contains six planting beds filled with colorful perennials and roses.
  - You will also find a laburnum covered pergola, a topiary wall, a bog garden established in 1997 and an excellent example of a Ha-Ha.
  - Note: This is a work in progress but it is a good example of an urban garden. A great deal of time and money is being spent to restore this garden and it is worth the visit.

The quaint city garden at G. White House.

The extraordinary pergola at West Dean will azae you.

## WEST DEAN GARDENS

- Hours of Admission: 11:00 to 5:00
- Location: outside town of West Dean
- What a discovery!
- Built in 1804, the present Gothic mansion was is unusual and distinctive for being faced entirely with flint.
- The present gardens, of approximately 30 acres, have undergone many changes over the years from the planting of large groups of trees in the late 18th century to the parkland of the early 19th century to the glorious pergola of the early 20th century.
- William James purchased the property in 1891 and commissioned architect and garden designer, Harold Peto to remodel the house and extended the garden.
- The parkland setting contains several wonderful old trees including two cedars planted by the Duke & Duchese of York in 1899 and one planted in 1901 by King Alphonso of Spain. One of the three cedar of Lebanon trees planted in 1748 still survives.
- A lovely pond, lush planting and a charming thatched roof garden house highlight the terraced sunken garden.
- From the sunken garden, stone steps take you up to the most fabulous pergola you will ever see. The 100 meter long pergola wrapped with roses, clematis and wisteria was designed by Harold Peto. Lovely borders line both sides of the stone pathway which is interrupted in the middle by a formal lily pond. As you continue on to the end of the pergola you will come to a stone garden house. The pergola required extensive restoration after the 1987 storm.
- The walled garden, virtually intact from its Victorian heyday, gives a visitor the opportunity to experience the garden organization that provisioned the needs of a prosperous household.
- Devastated by the 1987 storm, the 170 meter Woodland walk lost over 60 mature oaks and beeches. The area has since been replanted.
- Edward James created a charitable trust here in 1964 that founded a college teaching a wide range of traditional arts and crafts.
- Note: The visitors center, gift shop and tea room are in a new building which was designed in the old style and fits in very nicely. A great place to stop for lunch or tea.

## HINTON AMPNER GARDEN (N.T.)
- Hours of Admission: 1:30 to 5:30
- Location: 1 mile west of Bramdean on A272
  - This Georgian house was built in the late 18th century. Although it has been changed several times over the years, it has retained its Georgian beauty. The property was in the Dutton family for nearly 400 years until it was bequeathed to the National Trust in 1985.
  - Set in Hampshire countryside, this garden was redesigned and extended in the 1940's and combines a formal design with lovely informal plantings.
  - Off the back of the house is a stone terrace with a great display of rock roses and other sun-loving, drought tolerant plants.
  - The Sunken Garden, created in the 1930's, provides a lovely display in spring and summer.
  - Two wonderful spinx sculptures adorn the stairway leading to the Lily Pond. Here you will find a long bed of "Iceberg" roses under planted with a deep pink diascia
  - If you happen to be there at the right time (mid to late June) there is a charming philadelphus walk, the fragrance is overwhelming.

  - One of the best collections of hedge and topiary clippings. Enjoy the old mushroom topiaries on the terrace.
  - The area by the church comes alive in the early spring. Boxwood hedges and clipped cone shaped yews enclose the beauty of flowering cherries, bluebells and daffodils.
  - After suffering greatly in the storms of 1987 & 1990, the gardens have undergone five years of restoration and are now flourishing.

Hinton Ampner

## UPPARK (N.T.)
- Hours of Admission: 12:00 to 5:30
- Location: 5 miles southeast of Petersfield on B2146
  - H.G. Wells spent his early years here, his mother was housekeeper from 1880 to 1892.
  - Humphry Repton began improvements to the garden and house in 1810. He created a terraced area behind the house. It has disappeared now but if you visit Hinton Ampner first, you will have a picture of how this terraced area might have looked.
  - For more information, see page 103 under "Garden Descriptions".

**OTHER GARDENS IN THE AREA:** JANE AUSTEN'S HOUSE, GREATHAM MILL GARDEN

# TOUR #9
## MAP

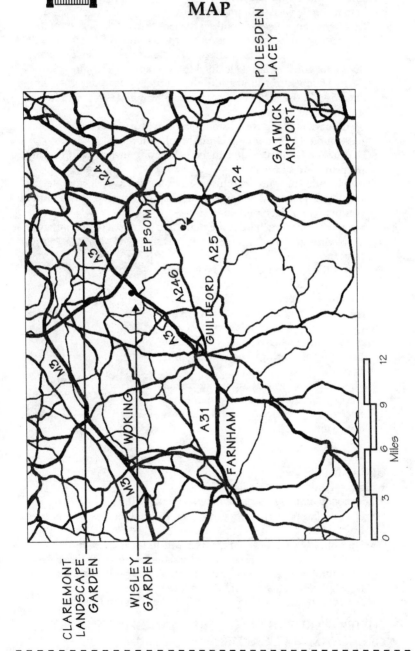

# TOUR #9

### * WISLEY GARDENS
### * POLESDEN LACEY
### * CLAREMONT LANDSCAPE GARDEN

## • MONDAY THROUGH SATURDAY •

In the 20th century garden at Polesden Lacey you will delight in the marvelous color from perennial borders, a double sided peony walk and a formal rose garden. The Royal Horticultural Society Garden at Wisley provides many interesting ideas for your own garden. The terraced lily pond and fabulous rock garden are only two. One of the earliest surviving landscape gardens, Claremont was touched by several of the great names in garden design from the 18th century. You will need up to two hours each at all three gardens. Travel time between Polesden Lacey and Wisley is 30 minutes. Travel time between Wisley and Claremont is 20 minutes.

### POLESDEN LACEY (N.T.)
- Hours of Admission: 11:00 to sunset
- Location: 5 miles northwest of Dorking
  - Joseph Bonsor built the elegant 1820's Regency villa and also planted 20,000 trees.
  - The house was remodeled in 1906 by Captain & Mrs. Greville. The architecture is very interesting with a widows walk, tower and pillared side porch. The Grevilles were also responsible for the development of most of the garden you see today. You will find 17 acres with fine views to the surrounding countryside.
  - In 1923 future King George VI and Queen Elizabeth spent part of their honeymoon here.
  - There is a series of rooms around the house that include bearded irises and a 100 foot double sided peony walk.
  - The walled garden has a long (450 feet) border filled with perennials and climbers. Follow this border to an urn with a ram's head and fruit, turn the corner and find another border with a fine garden house at the end.
  - A rustic pergola covered with Edwardian rambling roses highlights the large rose garden. Boxwoods, blue geraniums and lavenders define the beds of roses. The design is formal and the planting is fairly new. You have hundreds of roses to inspect.
  - Look for the beech and lime avenues, the thatched bridge and several interesting statues and garden ornaments including a cherub sundial.
  - Left to the National Trust in 1942.
  - Note: Mrs. Greville was the "hostess with the mostest" and in the house you will find a wonderful collection of silver and porcelain.

This fearce looking creature stands guard at Polesden Lacey.

## CLAREMONT LANDSCAPE GARDEN (N.T.)

- Hours of Admission: 10:00 to 6:00
- Location: south edge of Esher, east side of A307
  - One of earliest surviving English landscape gardens, Claremont was one of the most famous gardens in Europe during the 18th Century.
  - It was begun by John Vanbrugh who purchased the site in 1708, further developed by Charles Bridgeman and extended and naturalized by William Kent and "Capability" Brown between 1711 and 1774.
  - The glorious turf amphitheater that looks down on the lake was designed by Charles Bridgeman in 1726.
  - Rhododendrons surround the lake and island pavilion built by William Kent. Relax and watch the black swans swim peacefully by.
  - VanBrugh built the splendid "medieval" style belvedere.
  - "Capability" Brown was also commissioned to rebuild the house and make improvements to the grounds.
  - The 50 acre estate was acquired by the National Trust in 1949 and, with donations from several sources, restored to its former glory between 1975 & 1980.
  - Note: Not fancy but a historical landscape typical of 18th century. Busy on Sundays and Bank Holidays.

**OTHER GARDENS IN THE AREA:** CLANDON PARK, HATCHLANDS PARK

## WISLEY GARDEN

- Hours of Admission: 10:00 to 7:00
- Location: off A3 near Woking
  - This is the world famous 240 acre garden of the Royal Horticultural Society.
  - It was begun in the 1870's when Mr. G.F. Wilson purchased 60 acres and created the famous wild garden and constructed the ponds.
  - The Society moved here in 1904 and retained the wild garden, specimen trees and shrubs.
  - A great collection of rhododendrons and azaleas were planted on Battleston Hill starting in 1937.
  - A large terraced lily pond is filled with hundreds of water lilies all precisely labeled. The design is fabulous and might give you some good ideas for your own garden.
  - The extensive rock garden built up the side of a hill was constructed in 1911. As you wind your way up the path, you can inspect a terrific collection of plants while you listen to the water falls tumbling over the large boulders that form the backbone of the garden.
  - Surrounded by hedges of hornbeam and rosemary, the herb garden has a sundial at its center with four paths radiating from it. Of the four sections, one is devoted to culinary herbs, another to aromatic, the third to medicinal and the fourth to dye plants and folklore associations.
  - The huge rose garden is divided into four planting beds set up by color (red, pink, white & yellow). You will find all sorts of roses from climbers on the wooded trellises to tree roses to shrubs to teas. Fabulous climbing roses also cover the rope trellises lining both sides.
  - Among the other features you will find are a formal rose garden, an alpine meadow full of wild flowers and bulbs in the spring and two walled gardens designed by Geoffrey Jellicoe.
  - There are two restaurants, a picnic area, a visitor center which contains the world's best selection of gardening books and a garden center with over 8500 varieties of plants for sale.
  - Note: This place is a must but it can get a little crazy! Thousands of visitors stop here every day. Best time to visit would be during the week.

Wisley Garden

# TOUR #10
## MAP

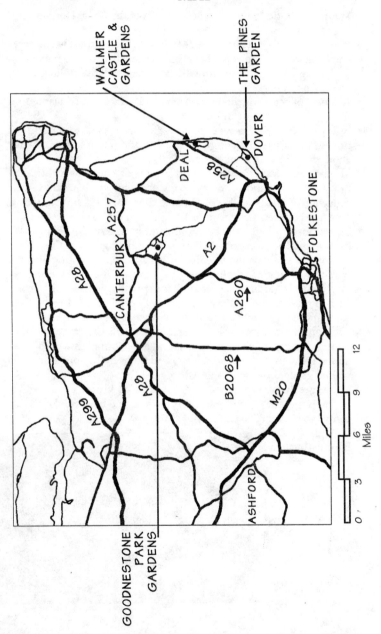

WALMER CASTLE & GARDENS

THE PINES GARDEN

DOVER

DEAL

A258

CANTERBURY A257

A2

FOLKESTONE

A28

A260

B2068

M20

A299

A28

ASHFORD

GOODNESTONE PARK GARDENS

0 3 6 9 12
Miles

# TOUR #10

* GOODNESTONE PARK GARDENS
* WALMER CASTLE
* THE PINES

## • DAILY EXCEPT TUESDAY & SATURDAY •

The white cliffs of Dover provide a backdrop for the garden at The Pines. This small seaside garden has a lovely lake with lush planting and a terrific rock garden. One hour is needed here. Now travel up the coast to Walmer Castle, a 16th century historic fortress with bright herbaceous borders and very interesting yew hedges. If you tour the castle, two hours will be needed here. I saved the best for last. The woodland garden at Goodnestone Park is an ideal setting for many lovely flowering shrubs but your real pleasure will be in exploring the glorious walled gardens. The village church provides the background for three rooms rich with the colors of perennials and roses. Relax and enjoy at least two hours here. Travel time between The Pines and Walmer is 20 minutes. Travel time between Walmer and Goodnestone is 40 minutes.

### THE PINES

- Hours of Admission: 10:00 to 5:00
- Location: 4.5 miles northeast of Dover; Beach Rd. in St. Margaret's Bay
  - A 6 acre seaside garden established in 1969.
  - As you stroll across a large lawn area, turn, look back and you will see the wonderful white cliffs of Dover.
  - A small lake is edged with lush water plants and colorful perennials. Wooden benches give you the opportunity to relax and enjoy feeding the ducks.
  - On the side of the hill just behind the lake there is a terrific rock garden. Water tumbles over the large rocks to form soothing waterfalls and a large collection of rock type plants grow out of nooks and crannies. I would say the inspiration came from the fantastic rock garden at Wisley.
  - You will find a statue of Winston Churchill that was dedicated by his son in 1972.
  - Note: Parking is in the street and is very limited.

The village church towers above the glorious gardens at Goodnestone Park.

## GOODNESTONE PARK GARDENS

- Hours of Admission; 11:00 to 5:00
- Location: south of Canterbury off B2046
  - The brick house, home of Lord FitzWalter's family since it was built about 1704, went through extensive remodeling in the late 18th century and again in the mid 19th century.
  - Fourteen acres of 18th century parkland is presently being extensively restored.
  - Terraced lawns to the east and west of the house have remained unchanged for nearly 300 years.
  - A grand avenue of red-twigged limes extends for approximately 200 yards was planted in 1984.
  - Walk through the 2-1/2 acre Woodland Garden and find some nice surprises. It is an ideal setting for acidic soil-loving plants such as rhododendrons, azaleas, hydrangeas and magnolias.
  - Be patient, follow the white arrows and you will soon come upon the glorious 18th century walled garden. The village church and 15th century Dower house provide a wonderful background for these colorful gardens. There is a series of three rooms containing a superb collection of old fashioned roses, herbaceous plants and climbers. The first consists of old fashioned roses, the second, borders of perennials and the third, tidy rows of vegies and fruit trees edged by clipped hedges and complimented by mixed borders the full length of the central path.
  - Most of the plants are raised at Goodnestone.
  - Jane Austen often visited, her brother Edward was married to the 3rd Baronet's daughter.
  - Note: What a surprise! This walled garden is one of the prettiest I've ever seen. Lots of photo opportunities. There is a cricket field near the entrance. See if you can figure that game out!

## WALMER CASTLE

- Hours of Admission: 10:00 to 6:00
- Location: on coast south of Walmer on A258
  - A 16th century castle, the Dover coastline, history and a lovely garden, that's what you will find here.
  - The fortress was built in 1540 by Henry VIII as a part of his coastal defenses but, more recently, it has been used as a domestic residence by the Queen Mother and the Duke of Wellington.
  - Much of the garden was laid out by Lady Hester Stanhope in the late 18th Century.
  - At the back of the castle you will find a colorful double sided herbaceous border backed by yew hedges clipped in the tortured shape of rocks and stones or...some terrible monster, use your imagination.
  - There is a small rose garden, a meadow with spring planting, a nicely maintained kitchen and cutting garden and a moat, once filled with water, now filled with plants.
  - You may even find time to play a little croquet on the lawn.
  - Note: Take a little time to tour the castle. It is occasionally occupied by the Queen Mother when she is fulfilling her role as Lord Warden of the Sinkport.

Colorful kitchen and cutting gardens
highlight Walmer Castle.

# TOUR #11
## MAP

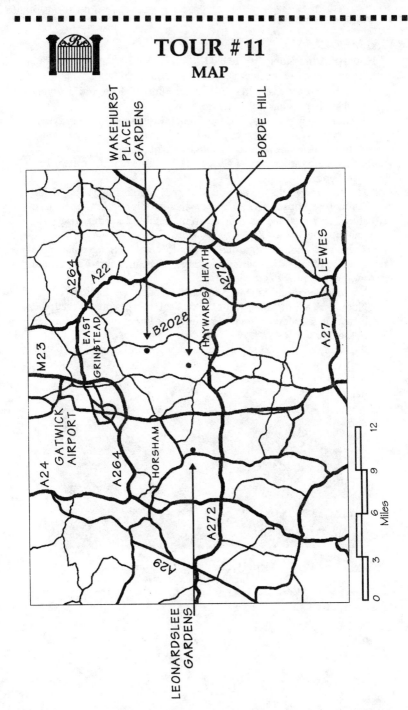

WAKEHURST PLACE GARDENS

BORDE HILL

LEWES

A264

A22

HAYWARDS HEATH

A272

EAST GRINSTEAD

B2028

M23

A27

GATWICK AIRPORT

A24

A264

HORSHAM

A272

A29

LEONARDSLEE GARDENS

0    3    6    9    12
        Miles

58

# TOUR #11

### * BORDE HILL
### * LEONARDSLEE GARDENS
### * WAKEHURST PLACE GARDENS
## • DAILY •

In this collection of beautiful woodland gardens you will find glorious displays of flowering shrubs and ornamental trees. Leonardslee also boasts seven lovely lakes and an unusual rock garden that is a fantasy of color with Kurume azaleas and dwarf rhododendrons. At Wakehurst Place two additional features are a delightful lush wetland garden and a walled garden with a charming sculpture of a child. You will also enjoy the fabulous views of the countryside and traditional style rose garden at Borde Hill. Up to two hours are needed at each garden. Travel time between Leonardslee and Borde Hill is 35 minutes. Travel time between Borde Hill and Wakehurst is 20 minutes.

## BORDE HILL GARDENS
* Hours of Admission: 10:00 to 6:00
* Location: 1.5 miles north of Haywards Heath

   * One of Sussex largest gardens, the primary character of the 400 acres is primarily informal woodlands. The rhododendrons, azaleas, magnolias and camellias are brilliant and gorgeous in May.
   * Much of the interior of the house is the original Elizabethan style dating from the early 17th Century but the outer appearance is 20th Century.
   * Take a few minutes to enjoy the view of the countryside from the back of the house, it is truly fabulous!
   * Robert Stephenson Clarke, who helped finance plant hunting expeditions, began planting in the 1890's and created an arboretum in the grand scale with many rare and unusual trees and shrubs.
   * The newly planted rose garden was done in the traditional style with boxwood hedges and catmint and lavenders along the edges. A nice collection of David Austin roses.
   * The Bride's Pool contains a good collection of water lilies and colorful border of penstemons
   * One of the many gardens that suffered terribly by the storm of 1987, Borde Hill is recovering.
   * Note: I was interested in the blue rose trellises. My husband and I are always looking for new ways of displaying our own roses. Are you?

This charming
fountain can be found
in the walled garden
at Wakehurst Place.

## WAKEHURST PLACE GARDEN (N.T.)

- Hours of Admission: 10:00 to 4:00
- Location: 1.5 miles northwest of Ardingly on B2028
  - The Elizabethan house, built in 1590 of Sussex sandstone, and 500 acres were purchased by Gerald Loder in 1903. He was responsible for creating the garden over the next 30 years. His older brother, Edmund Loder, created the gardens at Leonardslee.
  - This magnificent woodland garden is particularly noted for its rare trees and flowering shrubs and provides a spectacular display of rhododendrons and azaleas.
  - In the Wetland Garden you will find a delightful collection of plants selected for their foliage contrasts. Edges are completely enclosed by irises, cattails, primroses and skunk cabbage.
  - Look for the walled garden with clipped yews and a charming fountain sculpture of a child playing horns, a heather garden and a rock garden where magnolias, maples and dogwoods flourish.
  - The property was bequeathed to the National Trust in 1963 who then leased it to the Royal Botanic Gardens at Kew for scientific botanical and conservation research.
  - In the storms of 1987 and 1990 more than 15,000 trees were lost. Although tragic, it did allow for the planting of new and different varieties of trees.
  - Note: There is a fair amount of walking required.

## LEONARDSLEE GARDENS

- Hours of Admission: 10:00 to 6:00
- Location: 4 miles southeast of Horsham on A281
  - One of largest and most spectacular woodland gardens in England, it gets its name from the forest near by, the St. Leonards's Forest.
  - The 80 acres of gardens were laid out by Sir Edmund Loder between 1889 and 1920 (still in the Loder family). His younger brother Gerald Loder created the gardens at Wakehurst Place.
  - Panoramic views of the countryside can be enjoyed from the Georgian style house that was built in 1855.
  - Long descending paths carry you to a series of seven lakes at the bottom of the valley. The banks are richly planted with ornamental trees and shrubs.
  - You will find one of finest collections of mature camellias, rhododendrons and azaleas which are world famous for their spring display.
  - Conditions are perfect for growing these spring flowering shrubs. Centuries of leaf mold have created an ideal acid soil and the woodland setting provides shade during the hottest parts of the day and shelter against cold winter winds.
  - The Rock Garden, laid out in 1900, is one of the most unusual I've ever seen. It is a fantasy of color in May with Kurume azaleas and dwarf rhododendrons. Large natural rocks and a special concrete mixture have been used to create a very natural look.
  - The Alpine House has 400 different alpine plants in natural rocky setting.
  - Look for the superb exhibit of Bonsai in the walled courtyard.
  - Don't be surprised to see wallabies hopping around the garden.
  - Note: For the best color visit in April and May.

The rock garden at Leonardslee Gardens.

**OTHER GARDENS IN THE AREA:** NYMANS GARDENS, SHEFFIELD PARK GARDENS, STANDEN

# TOUR #12
## MAP

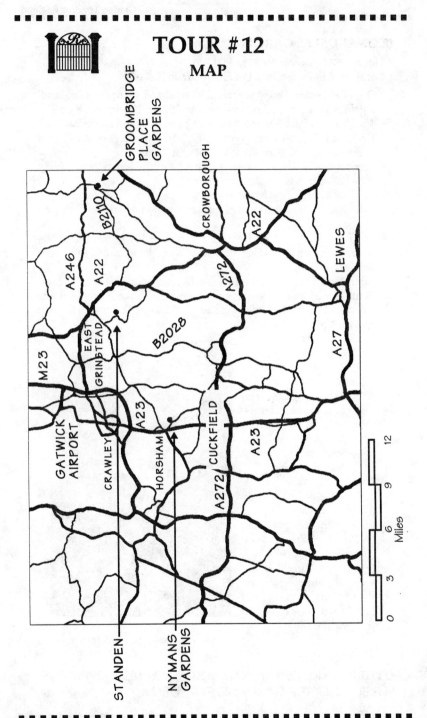

# TOUR #12

## * GROOMBRIDGE PLACE GARDENS
## * NYMANS GARDENS
## * STANDEN

# • WEDNESDAY THROUGH SUNDAY •

The romantic and picturesque ruins at Nymans provide a wonderful backdrop for colorful walled gardens and several unusual topiaries. A short visit to the house is a must. You will find a real gem at Groombridge Place. You can picture Sherlock Holmes strolling through the 17th century walled garden and inspecting the Shi Shi Dogs of War in the Oriental garden. From the furnishings in the house to the terraced gardens, William Morris and the Arts and Crafts Movement are in evidence at Standen. At least two hours are needed at each garden. Travel time between Nymans and Standen is 1 hour. Travel time between Standen and Groombridge is 40 minutes.

## STANDEN (N.T.)

- Hours of Admission: 12:30 to 6:00
- Location: 2 miles south of East Grinstead off B2110

  - A testimony to the ideals of Arts & Crafts Movement, the house was designed by Philip Webb in 1892 for the Beale family. Webb, a friend of William Morris, used local materials such as brick, timber, tile & stone.
  - The house contains original Morris & Co. furnishings.
  - The Beale family developed the garden in a fairly informal style in keeping with the style of the house.
  - When the National Trust took it over in 1972, they found it overgrown and neglected. It has been carefully restored to the late 19th century charm.
  - The steeply sloping site provides several levels of charming gardens that are connected by flights of steps with fabulous views across the Medway Valley.
  - The house terraces are brilliant with summer flowers, wild flowers and native orchids are planted in the upper lawns and grass walks lead to summerhouse and gazebo.
  - Although lovely in all seasons, spring is the best time to visit for the marvelous collection of rhododendrons, azaleas and woodland flowers.

## GROOMBRIDGE PLACE GARDENS

- Hours of Admission: 10:00 to 6:00
- Location: 4 miles southwest of Tunbridge Wells on B2110
  - This 17th century classical mansion and gardens were built by Philip Packer, a friend of the famous architect Sir Christopher Wren. The house is virtually unaltered since it was built during the restoration around 1660. The medieval moat that encircles the house dates from 1239.
  - Sir Arthur Conan Doyle, author of Sherlock Holmes, was a frequent visitor. As a matter of fact, in his story "Valley of Fear", the manor house he speaks of is Groombridge.
  - This is a real gem built in a series of rooms. The structure, yew hedges and stone walls, is old but restoration of the planting has taken place over the last few years. A good example is the 17th Century walled gardens.
  - Planted in 1994, the knot garden was inspired by the design of the 16th century paneling found in the house. You will find an astrolobe in the center and a sculpture of an old English couple enjoying the afternoon.
  - The Oriental garden is guarded by ancient Shi Shi Dogs of War. The borders are filled with soft colored perennials and have an Oriental flare. Some of the Japanese maples you will see are over 100 years old.
  - Over 20 species of wild flowers are found on Wild Flower Hill.
  - 3000 trees were planted recently to replace those lost in the storm of 1987.
  - Notes: How about a game of chess! Another idea for rose trellises. The gardeners are proud of their accomplishments and are quite willing to chat.

Ancient Shi Shi Dogs
of War guard the
Oriental Garden at
GroombridgePlace.

## NYMANS GARDEN (N.T.)

- Hours of Admission: 11:00 to 7:00
- Location: 4.5 miles south of Crawley
  - Ludwig Messel purchased the property with its Regency house and stand of cedar trees in 1890. He added the conservatory and Italianate tower and, in 1895, began developing the gardens.
  - Two of Messel's friends, Gertrude Jekyll & William Robinson, helped him create the 30 acres of formality mixed with informality.
  - This strong, essentially 20th Century design, contains plants, shrubs and trees from all over the world.
  - Some of the first heather gardens in the country were laid out here in 1903.
  - The sunken garden with its terrific Japanese lanterns and stone pergola built in 1903 was covered with wisteria imported from Japan in 1904. Severely damaged in the great storm, the pergola was restored in 1990 and replanted with young wisteria, clematis and rambling roses.
  - Messel's son rebuilt the house in Jacobean style but sadly, it was gutted by fire in 1947. It stands as a romantic and picturesque ruin.
  - The Walled Garden has colorful double borders of annuals & perennials, ornamental trees and shrubs, an Italian red marble fountain in the center and four unusual crown-shaped yew topiaries.
  - 147 varieties of old fashion roses fill the patterned beds of the large rose garden. Paths are edged with catmint and blue and white geraniums.
  - You will also find a wonderful dovecote, old turtle shaped topiaries, a well-labeled fushia garden and magnificently clipped yew hedges.
  - In spring there are carpets of daffodils, bluebells, tulips and forget-me-nots. In autumn the glorious color of Japanese maples is everywhere.
  - The devastating storm of 1987 destroyed 486 mature trees including the giant Monkey Puzzle tree and many other fine specimens.
  - Bequeathed to the National Trust in 1954.
  - Note: Follow the arrows and enjoy a pleasant walk and outstanding views of the countryside. On a clear day you can see 50 miles. A small portion of the house was occupied until 1992, take a few minutes to visit.

Nymans Gardens

**OTHER GARDENS IN THE AREA:** LEONARDSLEE GARDES, WAKEHURST PLACE GARDENS, BORDE HILL

# TOUR #13
## MAP

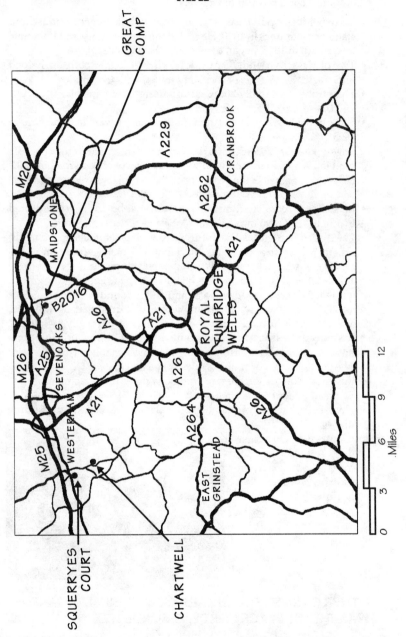

# TOUR #13

### * CHARTWELL
### * GREAT COMP
### * SQUERRYES COURT

## • WEDNESDAY, SATURDAY, SUNDAY •

If you are a student of World War II history as I am, you will thoroughly enjoy your visit to Winston Churchill's home at Chartwell. History is everywhere, in the charming house, the superb views, the fascinating paintings and best of all, in the lovely gardens. Two to three hours are needed here. The Warde family is taking great care to restore the gardens at Squerryes Court to their 17th century formality and charm. You will find several interesting features including an intricate partierre. Great Comp is a 20th century garden designed in a formal terraced style at the house with paths that lead you out to a more informal woodland area. One to two hours each are needed at Squerryes and Great Comp. Travel time between Chartwell and Squerryes is 15 minutes. Travel time between Squerryes and Great Comp is 40 minutes.

### SQUERRYES COURT

- Hours of Admission: 2:00 to 6:00
- Location: half mile west of Westerham off A25
  - This wonderful William & Mary manor house built in 1681 was purchased by the Warde family in 1731 and remains in the family today.
  - The 15 acres of historic gardens were originally laid out in a formal Anglo-Dutch style in 1709.
  - In the mid 18th Century the landscape was changed to the more natural style that was in fashion. Straight lines were out and all the formal plantings were swept away. At this time the lake was enlarged to what you see today.
  - The Warde family is in the process of restoring the 18th century formality and charm using original plans and a 1719 Badeslade print as guides. The intricate partierres were planted in 1989 according to the old print. The borders and yew hedges were planted in 1990. The current project is the woodland area.
  - Most of the large trees that created the hornbeam avenue were destroyed in the great storm, they were replanted in 1992.
  - In the house you will find an important collection of Italian, 18th Century English and 17th Century Dutch paintings.
  - Note: A good example of a privately owned garden under restoration. It demonstrates the time, money and care that is needed for such a project. There is much to see.

■■■■■■■■■■■■■■■■■■■■■■■■■■■■■■■■■■■■■■■■■■■■■■

Recently
restored
partierre at
Squerryes
Court.

## GREAT COMP

- Hours of Admission: 11:00 to 6:00
- Location: 2 miles east of Borough Green, B2016 off A20

  - There is a 17th century house and a seven acre garden that was developed over the last 40 years by Mr. & Mrs. Cameron.
  - The style is natural and informal with lawns and paths leading visitors through a plantsman's collection of trees, shrubs, heathers and herbaceous plants.
  - The backbone of the garden may be mature lime trees but you will also find over 3000 different plants.
  - Around the house you will find more formal terraced gardens of fragrant lavenders, perennials and roses.
  - Note: Some of the features may be a little hoaky but overall the garden is very interesting.

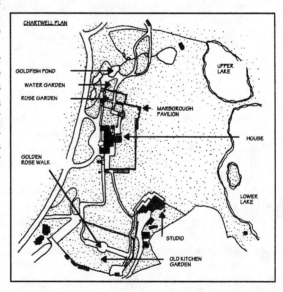

■ ■ ■ ■ ■ ■ ■ ■ ■ ■ ■ ■ ■ ■ ■ ■ ■ ■ ■ ■ ■ ■ ■ ■ ■ ■ ■ ■ ■ ■ ■

■■■■■■■■■■■■■■■■■■■■■■■■■■■■■■■■■■■■■■■■■■■

## CHARTWELL (N.T.)

- Hours of Admission: 11:00 to 5:30
- Location: 2 miles south of Westerham, forking left off B2026
  - The home of Winston Churchill from 1924 until his death in 1964. It was closed during most of World War II because it was too conspicuous from the air. You can feel the history.
  - Origins of the house are from the 16th century. Henry VIII was said to have stayed here while courting Anne Boleyn at Hever Castle. It was enlarged and remodeled in the mid-19th century to an essentially Victorian style and again remodeled for Churchill between 1922-1924.
  - Churchill was captivated by Chartwell from the very first. The landscape and sweeping views over the Weald of Kent provided countless scenes for his paintbrush and many wonderful places to relax and think. Can you picture him strolling through the garden or just sitting by the goldfish pond?
  - The garden was planned, created and in some cases built by the Churchills. The walls of the vegetable garden were built largely by his hands.
  - Lady Churchill laid out the lovely walled rose garden in the 1920's. It contains mostly teas with wisteria and mixed borders along the walls.
  - The water garden includes the colorful goldfish pond (one of Churchill's favorite spots) and a chain of ponds that are connected by waterfalls and rock work. Behind the pool are white foxgloves and blue anchusa.
  - Enjoy the superb views of the countryside while you relax on the arched benches in the terraced lawn. From here you can also see...
  - The Golden Rose Walk which was created in 1958 by their children to commemorate the Churchill's Golden Wedding. You will find yellow and golden color roses under planted by purple catmint.
  - The beech woods that sheltered the valley was devastated in the storm of 1987, 70-80 percent of the trees were lost.
  - Note: Charming and simple country style garden. Visit the house and studio for their historic value and for the fabulous art collection. Look for Mary Churchill's playhouse. Can be quite busy.

## OTHER GARDENS IN THE AREA: HEVER CASTLE, PENSHURST PLACE, IGHTHAM MOTE, EMMETTS GARDENS

■■■■■■■■■■■■■■■■■■■■■■■■■■■■■■■■■■■■■■■■■

# TOUR #14
## MAP

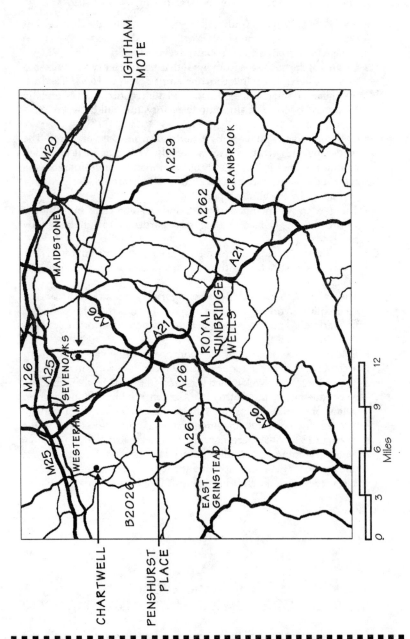

# TOUR #14

### * PENSHURST PLACE
### * IGHTHAM MOTE
### * CHARTWELL

## • WEDNESDAY, THURSDAY, SUNDAY •

Centuries of history will be found on this tour, from the 14th century King Arthur style manor house at Penshurst Place to the 15th century moated house at Ightham Mote to the charming 20th century home of Winston Churchill. The gardens at Ightham are being restored to their romantic 'Olde English' style. You will need one to two hours here. The lush and colorful walled gardens at Penshurst were created in the Elizabethan period and have changed little. The Churchills created the lovely rose gardens, a colorful water garden and the walled kitchen garden at Chartwell. Two to tree hours each will be needed at Penshurst and Chartwell. Travel time between Penshurst and Chartwell is 35 minutes. Travel time between Chartwell and Ightham is 45 minutes.

### IGHTHAM MOTE (N.T.)

• Hours of Admission: 12:00 to 5:30
• Location: 6 miles east of Sevenoaks off A25
  • Set in wooded valley, this moated manor house covers 650 years of history from the Medieval Great Hall (1430's) to the Victorian housekeepers room.
  • The Selby family bought it in 1591 and occupied it for the next 300 years.
  • Henry Robinson of Portland, Maine fell in love with the "Mote" as a young man. He bought it in 1953, made several repairs and lived here in the summers until his death at 93 in 1985.
  • Robinson bequeathed it to The National Trust who began one of the largest conservation & reconstruction programs ever undertaken; it will continue for several more years. This is a good example of the time and care The Trust takes in refurbishing these important historical properties.
  • Although never an extensive garden, many changes have taken place over the years. The most recent changes were influenced by the return to brilliant flower gardens and the Arts & Crafts Movement of the late 19th century. After absorbing these influences the garden emerged as the ideal "Olde English" garden.
  • The National Trust is seeking to restore the garden to that romantic charm. You will find a walled kitchen and cutting garden, large lawn area, colorful flower beds, paved fountain garden and a lily pool.
  • Note: I love these charming moated castles. This one is almost as nice as Baddesly Clinton.

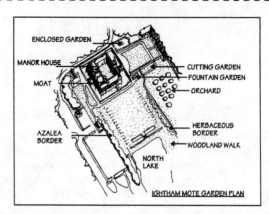

Inside the map/plan:
ENCLOSED GARDEN
MANOR HOUSE
MOAT
CUTTING GARDEN
FOUNTAIN GARDEN
ORCHARD
HERBACEOUS BORDER
WOODLAND WALK
AZALEA BORDER
NORTH LAKE
IGHTHAM MOTE GARDEN PLAN

## PENSHURST PLACE

- Hours of Admission: 11:00 to 6:00
- Location: 3 miles north of Tunbridge Wells
  - This well preserved King Arthur style, medieval manor house dates from 1341 and was made from sandstone, which is rare in this area. It has crenalated walls and the original chestnut roof timbers.
  - Home of the Sidney family since 1552, the gardens were laid out in their present style in the 16th Century.
  - Designed in a series of "rooms" and divided by a **mile** (that's right, a mile) of yew hedges. The rooms include the nut garden, a rose and lavender partierre surrounded by espalied nut trees; a theater garden, a union flag garden and a magnolia garden.
  - The ten acre brick walled garden has changed little since the Elizabethan period. No other walled ornamental garden on this scale survives in an English garden.
  - Within the walled garden you will find shrub and tree roses surrounded by barberries, lambs ears and Spanish lavender (a stunning combination); a 100 yard border of massed peonies surrounded by English lavender and backed by red leafed barberries and double sided herbaceous borders.
  - The large, simply planted Italian garden has a sunken parterre filled with boxwood hedges and roses that forms geometric patterns around an oval pool and fountain sculpture.
  - Note: A good place for tea on a warm afternoon under a big old red beech. There is a children's play area.

Penshurst Place

## CHARTWELL (N.T.)

- Hours of Admission: 11:00 to 5:30
- Location: 2 miles south of Westerham, forking left off B2026
  - The home of Winston Churchill from 1924 until his death in 1964, it was closed during most of World War II because it was too conspicuous from the air. You can feel the history.
  - Origins of the house are from the 16th century. Henry VIII was said to have stayed here while courting Anne Boleyn at Hever Castle. It was enlarged and remodeled in the mid-19th century to an essentially Victorian style and again remodeled for Churchill between 1922-1924.
  - Churchill was captivated by Chartwell from the very first. The landscape and sweeping views over the Weald of Kent provided countless scenes for his paintbrush and many wonderful places to relax and think. Can you see him wandering or just sitting by the goldfish pond?
  - The garden was planned, created and in some cases built by the Churchills. The walls of the vegetable garden were built largely by his hands.
  - Lady Churchill laid out the lovely walled rose garden in the 1920's. It contains mostly teas with wisteria and mixed borders along the walls.
  - The water garden includes the colorful goldfish pond (one of Churchill's favorite spots) and a chain of ponds that are connected by waterfalls and rock work. Behind the pool are white foxgloves and blue anchusa.
  - Enjoy the superb views of the countryside while you relax on the arched benches in the terraced lawn. From here you can also see-
  - The Golden Rose Walk which was created in 1958 by their children to commemorate the Churchill's Golden Wedding. You will find yellow and golden colored roses under planted by purple catmint.
  - The beech woods that sheltered the valley was devastated in the storm of 1987, 70-80 percent of the trees were lost.
  - Note: Charming and simple country style garden. Visit the house and studio for their historic value and for the fabulous art collection. Look for Mary Churchill's playhouse. Can be quite busy.

Chartwell

**OTHER GARDENS IN THE AREA:** SQUERRYES COURT, GREAT COMP, EMMETTS GARDEN, HEVER CASTLE

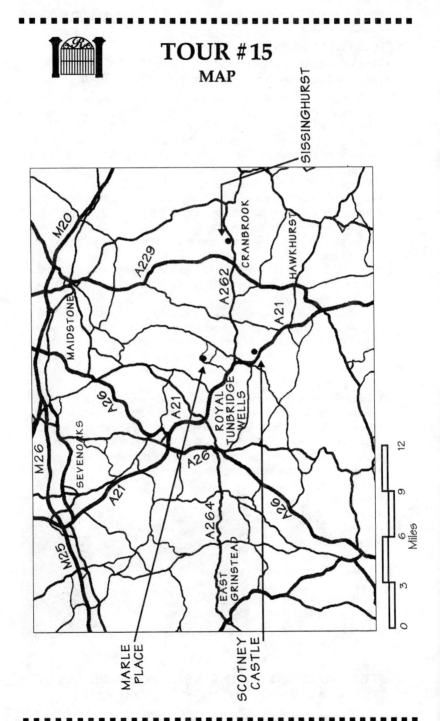

■■■■■■■■■■■■■■■■■■■■■■■■■■■■■■■■■■■■■■■■■■■■

# TOUR #15

### * SISSINGHURST GARDEN
### * SCOTTNEY CASTLE
### * MARLE PLACE

## • WEDNESDAY THROUGH SUNDAY •

A great masterpiece of 20th century garden design, Sissinghurst was created in a series of glorious garden 'rooms'. Inspect the color and design of each room and then view the complete layout from the 16th century brick tower. At least three hours will be needed here. The ruins of a romantic 14th century moated castle surrounded by a profusion of colorful shrubs and magnificent trees is the 'picturesque' view you will find at Scotney Castle. The privately owned garden at Marle Place contain several wonderful beds and borders planted for their color and for foliage contrasts. One to two hours each will be needed at Scotney and Marle. Travel time Between Marle and Scotney is 20 minutes. Travel time between Scotney and Sissinghurst is 45 minutes.

### MARLE PLACE

- Hours of Admission: 10:30 to 5:00
- Location: 8 miles southeast of Tonbridge
  - We happened on this garden a few years ago. It was quite a find!
  - A lovely 17th century red brick house is surrounded by a 10 acre privately owned plantsman's garden.
  - You will find a combination of hedged "rooms" and tree lined avenues.
  - The planting is not only colorful flowers but also some of the most outstanding contrasts in foliage color, size and shape that I've seen.
  - It is a garden of color, scent and sound throughout the seasons. The wonderful collection of plants provide the color and scent and the fountain, ornamental pool and ponds filled with ducks and geese provide the sounds.
  - A woodland area is planted with specimen trees and bordered by a stream that flows into two large ponds.
  - Look for the Victorian gazebo, a fabulous hydrangea (*petiolaris*) climbing on the house, an Edwardian rockery and several dogs chasing each other through the garden.

Marle Place

■■■■■■■■■■■■■■■■■■■■■■■■■■■■■■■■■■■■■■■■■■■■■ 75

The rondel highlights this view from the tower at Sissinghurst.

## SISSINGHURST GARDEN (N.T.)

- Hours of Admission: Tue-Fri 1:00 to 6:30, Sat & Sun 10:00 to 5:30
- Location: 7 miles northwest of Tenterden off A262
  - One of the great masterpieces of 20th century garden design created by Vita Sackville-West and her husband Harold Nicolson starting in the 1930's.
  - Only a small portion of the original buildings remain from the important 16th & 17th Century estate. There is the fine gate house c 1490 and the wonderful red brick Elizabethan tower c 1565 that provides panoramic views of the countryside and this world famous, 5.5 acre garden.
  - The couple worked in partnership to create the garden, Harold was responsible for the overall pattern and Vita for the detailed planting.
  - Designed in a series of garden "rooms", each one is quite different from the other. Rooms are linked by vistas, walks and hedged paths similar to the theme you will find at Hidcote Manor in Gloucestershire.
  - One of the most famous rooms is the White Garden where green and white variegated leaves and gray foliage provide a wonderful background for many shades of white flowers such as peonies, irises, roses and the smoke bush.
  - The famous herb garden, planted in 1938, is the oldest existing herb garden in England and has inspired herb gardens throughout Britain. Over 60 varieties of herbs were planted for their foliage since Vita was not keen on cooking.
  - You will also find a walled garden with terrific borders and climbing roses, a red border, an old orchard, a rondel and Vita's huge collection of old fashioned shrub and climbing roses.
  - See if you can find the fence lined with bright blue geraniums. It's one of my favorite spots.
  - A walk to the top of the tower is a must. You will get a wonderful look at the complete layout of the garden. Stairs are narrow and winding so be careful.
  - The property was passed to the National Trust in 1967.
  - Note: There are hundreds of photo opportunities here. Bring lots of film. Avoid weekends if you can or go early or late in the day. Timed Tickets are used during peak hours.

## SCOTNEY CASTLE (N.T.)

- Hours of Admission: Wed-Fri 11:00 to 6:00, Sat & Sun 2:00 to 6:00
- Location: 6 miles east of Tunbridge Wells on A21
  - One of the most romantic gardens you will visit! It is an excellent example of the picturesque period of landscape gardening.
  - In 1835 Edward Hussey III moved to Scotney and built a country house. The style of the 'new' house is Elizabethan built from the mellow sandstone quarried from the slope below.
  - Hussey hired William Sawrey Gilpin to design the area around the 'new' house which he sited on a terrace 25 meters above the old castle.
  - Gilpin also devised the spectacular, 'picturesque' views down to the Old Castle. The view includes a profusion of rhododendrons, azaleas and hundreds of magnificent trees which provide an unbelievable backdrop.
  - Climbing roses, wisteria and lilac cover the ruins of 14th century moated castle in colorful profusion.
  - This is not a formal or flower garden but you will find shrub roses, herbaceous plants and a small circular garden of herbs and cottage plants in courtyard.
  - An abundance of water lilies fill the moat while yellow irises and other water loving plants flourish around the edges.
  - A rock garden now grows in the quarry that provided the stone to build the house.
  - Here too, the storm of 1987 brought down many mature trees.
  - Given to the National Trust in 1970.
  - Note: I never tire of visiting this romantic old castle.

The romantic and wonderful Scotney Castle.

## OTHER GARDENS IN THE AREA: GREAT DIXTER, MERRIMENTS GARDEN

# TOUR #16
## MAP

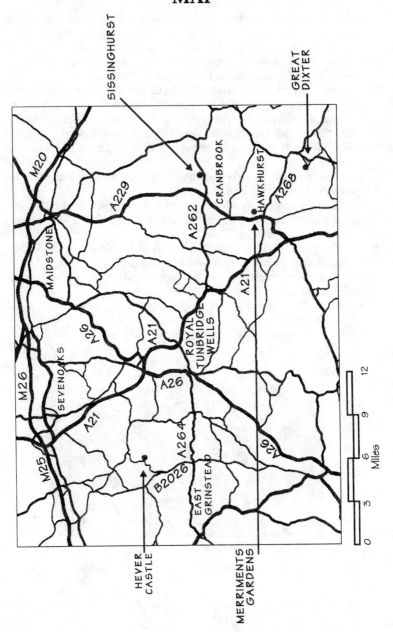

# TOUR #16

## * GREAT DIXTER
## * SISSINGHURST GARDENS
## * MERRIMENTS GARDENS

## • DAILY EXCEPT MONDAY •

A study in contrasts can be found by visiting the magnificent gardens at Sissinghurst and Great Dixter. Both created in the 20th century, Sissinghurst, created by Vita Sackville-West, is a series of formal garden 'rooms' filled with color and linked by vistas, walks and hedges while Great Dixter is the more 'free-spirited' creation of Christopher Lloyd. His famous Long Border is a glorious mixture of perennials and roses. Two to three hours each are needed at Sissinghurst and Great Dixter. Merriments is a fabulous collection of colorful mixed borders created over the last five years. There are many good ideas for your own garden here so two hours will be needed. Travel time between Sissinghurst and Great Dixter is 40 minutes. Travel time between Great Dixter and Merriments is 20 minutes.

### MERRIMENTS GARDENS

- Hours of Admission: 10:00 to 5:00
- Location: Hawkhurst Road, Hawkhurst
  - This four acre garden was developed over the last five years by a family of "amateurs". They obviously enjoy what they're doing and have a real sense of design since they started with bare ground and have created some of the most fabulous mixed borders I've seen.
  - There are spring borders and others designed to peak in the summer. Some were planted with a color theme such as blues and pinks or oranges and yellows and some were planted for their foliage contrasts.
  - Over 400 trees were planted, a large pond was dug and a stream was created.
  - The large pond flows into a creek that flows into another pond and all this is surrounded by a wonderful collection of bog plants with a small rock garden to one side.
  - A rustic pergola built from tree branches is covered with red roses.
  - One of the first areas you come upon is a series of blue trellises with roses climbing on them and perennial borders below. Does this remind you of Giverney?
  - The brown and white springer that romps around the garden reminded me of the one waiting at our home.
  - Note: We stayed in Hawkhurst for a few days this trip and happened upon this terrific new garden. Don't miss it! By the way, there is also a very nice nursery and people happy to answer questions.

Climb the tower
stairs and find the
best view of the
garden 'rooms'
at Sissinghurst.

## SISSINGHURST GARDEN (N.T.)

- Hours of Admission: Tue-Fri 1:00 to 6:30, Sat & Sun 10:00 to 5:30
- Location: 7 miles northwest of Tenterden off A262
  - One of the great masterpieces of 20th century garden design created by Vita Sackville-West and her husband Harold Nicolson starting in the 1930's.
  - Only a small portion of the original buildings remain from the important 16th & 17th Century estate. There is the fine gate house c 1490 and the wonderful red brick Elizabethan tower c 1565 that provides panoramic views of the countryside and this world famous, 5.5 acre garden.
  - The couple worked in partnership to create the garden, Harold was responsible for the overall pattern and Vita for the detailed planting.
  - Designed in a series of garden "rooms", each one is quite different from the other. Rooms are linked by vistas, walks and hedged paths similar to the theme you will find at Hidcote Manor in Gloucestershire.
  - One of the most famous rooms is the White Garden where green and white variegated leaves and gray foliage provide a wonderful background for many shades of white flowers such as peonies, irises, roses and the smoke bush.
  - The famous herb garden, planted in 1938, is the oldest existing herb garden in England and has inspired herb gardens throughout Britain. Over 60 varieties of herbs were planted for their foliage since Vita was not keen on cooking.
  - You will also find a walled garden with terrific borders and climbing roses, a red border, an old orchard, a rondel and Vita's huge collection of old fashioned shrub and climbing roses.
  - See if you can find the fence lined with bright blue geraniums. It's one of my favorite spots.
  - A walk to the top of the tower is a must. You will get a wonderful look at the complete layout of the garden. Stairs are narrow and winding so be careful.
  - The property was passed to the National Trust in 1967.
  - Note: There are hundreds of photo opportunities here. Bring lots of film. Avoid weekends if you can or go early or late in the day. Timed Tickets are used during peak hours.

## GREAT DIXTER

- Hours of Admission: 2:00 to 5:00
- Location: half mile north of Northiam off A28
  - Not far from Sissinghurst you will find this gem of the Arts and Crafts Movement. Quite a contrast!
  - Originally built in the 15th Century, it was restored and extended by Edwin Lutyens in the early 20th century for the new owner, Nathaniel Lloyd.
  - Lutyens' design characterizes the garden of today. He linked the house with the different levels of the garden by means of walls, terraces, steps and paths.
  - Nathanial Lloyd added many of the topiaries, including the big, old squirrels, and designed the lovely sunken garden with lily pond and climbing plants.
  - Mrs. Lloyd originally selected many of the plants that flourish in this garden but later one of her sons, plantsman and author Christopher Lloyd, applied his touch.
  - You will find a vigorous mixture of plants that give year round interest and enjoyment. The plants are selected for their foliage contrasts in addition to their flowers.
  - Christopher Lloyd, a pioneer of the mixed border, created the famous Long Border (200 ft. long and 15 ft. wide). Look for a glorious mixture of colorful perennials and roses that has an unusually long season of interest, from April to October.
  - The Meadow Garden, beautiful in spring, is a field of wild flowers and bulbs of all sorts started by Mrs. Lloyd who raised wild daffodils.

  - There are many other lovely features: brick arches in the walled garden, a kitchen garden with espalied trees, high terraces, and unusual clipped hedges and topiaries.
  - The reputation of Great Dixter is based on the reputation of Christopher Lloyd. He has spent a lifetime experimenting to create a garden for all the senses and for all the seasons.
  - Look for the oast house.
  - Note: Not quite what I expected-definitely "free-spirited"! A good contrast to Sissinghurst.

Great Dixter

**OTHER GARDENS IN THE AREA:** SCOTTNEY CASTLE, MARLE PLACE, HEVER CASTLE

# TOUR #17
## MAP

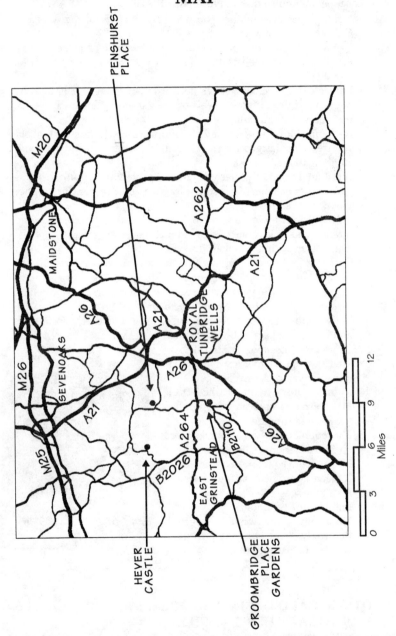

■■■■■■■■■■■■■■■■■■■■■■■■■■■■■■■■■■■■■■■■

# TOUR #17

## * GROOMBRIDGE PLACE GARDENS
## * PENSHURST PLACE
## * HEVER CASTLE

## • DAILY •

The beautiful gardens surrounding the 15th century castle at Hever Castle were created by American, William Astor. One of the most stunning features is the Italian garden which provides a backdrop for Astor's superb collection of sculpture and statuary. Yew hedges and stone walls provide the structure for the terrific series of rooms at Groombridge Place. A recently planted knot garden was inspired by a 16th century panel found in the house. A mile of yew hedges divide the garden 'rooms' at Penshurst Place. Within these rooms you will find a border of massed peonies, an unusual rose garden and a great place to stop for tea. Up to two hours are needed for each garden. Travel time between Groombridge and Penshurst is 15 minutes. Travel time between Penshurst and Hever is 20 minutes.

### PENSHURST PLACE

- Hours of Admission: 11:00 to 6:00
- Location: 3 miles north of Tunbridge Wells
  - This well preserved King Arthur style, medieval manor house dates from 1341 and was made from sandstone, which is rare in this area. It has crenalated walls and the original chestnut roof timbers.
  - Home of the Sidney family since 1552, the gardens were laid out in their present style in the 16th Century.
  - Designed in a series of "rooms" and divided by a **mile** (that's right, a mile) of yew hedges. The rooms include the nut garden, a rose and lavender partierre surrounded by espalied nut trees; a theater garden, a union flag garden and a magnolia garden.
  - The ten acre brick walled garden has changed little since the Elizabethan period. No other walled ornamental garden on this scale survives in an English garden.
  - Within the walled garden you will find shrub and tree roses surrounded by barberries, lambs ears and Spanish lavender (a stunning combination); a 100 yard border of massed peonies surrounded by English lavender and backed by red leafed barberries and double sided herbaceous borders.
  - The large, simply planted Italian garden has a sunken parterre filled with boxwood hedges and roses that forms geometric patterns around an oval pool and fountain sculpture.
  - Note: A good place for tea on a warm afternoon under a big old red beech. There is a children's play area.

■■■■■■■■■■■■■■■■■■■■■■■■■■■■■■■■■■■■■■■■

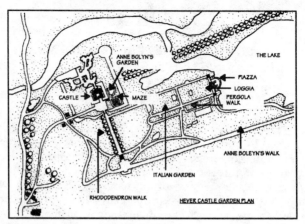

**HEVER CASTLE**

- Hours of Admission: 11:00 to 6:00
- Location: 3 miles southeast of Edenbridge between Sevenoaks and East Grinstead
  - Visit this romantic 15th Century moated castle and you are visiting one of the most beautiful gardens in England.
  - This was the Boleyn family home and the place Henry VIII's wife, Anne Boleyn, spent her childhood.
  - No record of the garden exists until American William Waldorf Astor bought the property in 1903. The 30 acres of formal gardens were planted between 1904 & 1908 during which as many as 1000 men were employed.
  - Aster had been American Minister in Rome where he gathered a remarkable collection of Roman antiquities & Renaissance sculpture and statuary. The four acre Italian garden provides a backdrop for this superb collection. You will find stone walls, yew hedges, colorful planting beds and a loggia embellished with an incredible fountain.
  - The loggia provides stunning views over the 35 acre lake which took 800 men to excavate.
  - Anne Boleyn's Garden is laid out in series of small gardens just as it would have been in the 15th century. You will find a Tudor herb garden, many varieties of roses and annuals that change from season to season. These gardens were replanted after the 1987 storm.
  - The gardens are a delight at any season. Thousands of daffodils and flowering trees bloom in the early spring, followed by azaleas and rhododendrons. Roses and perennials are in full bloom in the summer and the vibrant color of changing leaves bring the autumn alive.
  - Other features to look for are: the pergola walk intertwined with wisteria & roses and supported by laburnum and apple trees; an 80 foot square maze, planted in 1906, that now reaches 8 ft. in height; a chess garden with pieces sculpted out of golden yews.

Lovely flowers line
the crenalated walls at
Penshurst Place.

## GROOMBRIDGE PLACE GARDENS

- Hours of Admission: 10:00 to 6:00
- Location: 4 miles southwest of Tunbridge Wells on B2110
  - This 17th century classical mansion and gardens were built by Philip Packer, a friend of the famous architect Sir Christopher Wren. The house is virtually unaltered since it was built during the restoration around 1660. The medieval moat that encircles the house dates from 1239.
  - Sir Arthur Conan Doyle, author of Sherlock Holmes, was a frequent visitor. As a matter of fact, in his story "Valley of Fear", the manor house he speaks of is Groombridge.
  - This is a real gem built in a series of rooms. The structure, yew hedges and stone walls, is old but restoration of the planting has taken place over the last few years. A good example is the 17th Century walled gardens.
  - Planted in 1994, the knot garden was inspired by the design of the 16th century paneling found in the house. You will find an astrolobe in the center and a sculpture of an old English couple enjoying the afternoon.
  - The Oriental garden is guarded by ancient Shi Shi Dogs of War. The borders are filled with soft colored perennials and have an Oriental flare. Some of the Japanese maples you will see are over 100 years old.
  - Over 20 species of wild flowers are found on Wild Flower Hill.
  - 3000 trees were planted to replace those lost in the storm of 1987.

- Notes: How about a game of chess! Another idea for rose trellises. The gardeners are proud of their accomplishments and are quite willing to chat.

Groombridge Place

## OTHER GARDENS IN THE AREA: CHARTWELL, IGHTHAM MOTE, SCOTTNEY CASTLE

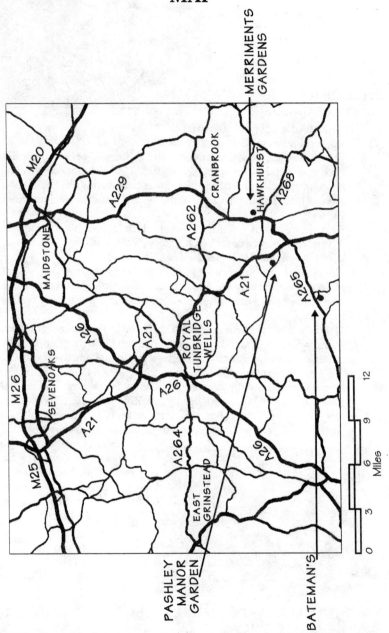

# TOUR #18

### * BATEMAN'S
### * PASHLEY MANOR GARDENS
### * MERRIMENTS GARDENS

## • TUESDAY, WEDNESDAY, SATURDAY •

The history of Kent includes many famous authors. One such is Bateman's, the home of Rudyard Kipling. The garden, with its pear and clematis pergola, lovely rose garden and large pond, was created by Kipling and his wife. Around the Tudor house at Pashley Manor you will find a terraced garden with magnificent views to the countryside and a lovely lake. You will also find a thriving kitchen garden lined with colorful perennials. Some of the most fabulous mixed borders I've ever seen were created over the last five years at Merriments. You should find several good ideas for your own garden. One to two hours each are needed for these three gardens. Travel time between Bateman's and Pashley is 20 minutes. Travel time between Pashley and Merriments is 20 minutes.

## MERRIMENTS GARDENS

- Hours of Admission: 10:00 to 5:00
- Location: Hawkhurst Road, Hawkhurst

  - This four acre garden was developed over the last five years by a family of "amateurs". They obviously enjoy what they're doing and have a real sense of design since they started with bare ground and have created some of the most fabulous mixed borders I've seen.
  - There are spring borders and others designed to peak in the summer. Some were planted with a color theme such as blues and pinks or oranges and yellows and some were planted for their foliage contrasts.
  - Over 400 trees were planted, a large pond was dug and a stream was created.
  - The large pond flows into a creek that flows into another pond and all this is surrounded by a wonderful collection of bog plants with a small rock garden to one side.
  - A rustic pergola built from tree branches is covered with red roses.
  - One of the first areas you come upon is a series of blue trellises with roses climbing on them and perennial borders below. Does this remind you of Giverney?
  - The brown and white springer that romps around the garden reminded me of the one waiting at our home.
  - Note: We stayed in Hawkhurst for a few days this trip and happened upon this terrific new garden. Don't miss it! By the way, there is also a very nice nursery and people happy to answer questions.

This pond at
Bateman's was
designed by
Rudyard
Kipling.

## BATEMAN'S (N.T.)

- Hours of Admission: 11:00 to 5:30
- Location: half mile south of Burwash off A265
  - The Jacobean house, built in 1634, and ten acres of gardens are located in one of Sussex's most beautiful valleys.
  - This was the home of Rudyard Kipling from 1902 to 1936 and much of the house remains as it was in Kipling's time including his study.
  - Kipling and his wife created much of the garden. It was laid out to complement the house in a series of outdoor rooms edged by stone walls and tall yew and box hedges.
  - Old pears interspersed with clematis are trained to form a long pergola. There are borders on each side with red brick paving.
  - Enjoy the lovely rose garden with a fountain as the focal point. The structure and paving in this area is quite old but the planting was done in the last couple years.
  - Pass through the gate west of the rose garden and the planting becomes less formal with flowering trees and shrubs and carpet of bulbs in the spring.
  - Large pond with magnificent water lilies was originally designed for boating and swimming by Kipling's children.
  - The herb garden is 80 ft. by 6 ft. and contains 80 different herbs massed together as they would be in a grand herbaceous border.
  - You may want to wander down to the mill house by the river or spend a few minutes relaxing in one of the garden benches tucked away in the clipped hedges. The benches are cozy and are designed to protect you on a windy day.
  - Note: If you are an antique car buff, look for Kipling's 1928 Rolls Royce.

■ ■ ■ ■ ■ ■ ■ ■ ■ ■ ■ ■ ■ ■ ■ ■ ■ ■ ■ ■ ■ ■ ■ ■ ■ ■ ■ ■ ■ ■ ■ ■ ■ ■ ■ ■ ■ ■ ■ ■ ■ ■ ■ ■

## PASHLEY MANOR GARDENS

- Hours of Admission: 11:00 to 5:00
- Location: between Ticehurst and A21 on B2099
  - The Bolyn family owned the estate from 1453 to 1543 and it is probable that Anne spent time here as a child.
  - The house you see today is Tudor dating from 1553 with magnificent views of Brightling Beacon. The Georgian facade was added in 1720.
  - This eight acre 18th Century formal garden was created in the English romantic style. This structure remains but much of the planting is fairly new.
  - At first you enter the 'patio room' with red brick walls, lovely borders and views to a lake and the scenic countryside. A perfect spot to relax and enjoy a cool gin & tonic.
  - Step down to find a real swimming pool. The same brick walls provide a backdrop for climbing roses, stone paving all around and a wonderful little greenhouse at one end.
  - A large thriving kitchen garden has a double border of perennials, annuals and roses along the path. You will find an unbelievable display of white foxgloves if you visit in early June.
  - Look for the rose garden with brick walls on three sides and a collection of old apple trees.
  - Take the woodland walk around the lake and enjoy the color of native rhododendrons and windows of opportunity to view two interesting fountains and the house.
  - Most of the specimen conifers that form a great deal of the structure of the garden were planted in the mid 19th century.
  - The house was unoccupied from 1922 to 1945 except for a brief time during World War II when it was occupied by troops and others driven there by falling bombs. Extensive restoration to both the house and garden were needed when the new owner purchased the property in 1945.

Charming little greenhouse
at Pashley Manor.

**OTHER GARDENS IN THE AREA:** SISSINGHURST GARDENS, GREAT DIXTER, SCOTTNEY CASTLE

■ ■ ■ ■ ■ ■ ■ ■ ■ ■ ■ ■ ■ ■ ■ ■ ■ ■ ■ ■ ■ ■ ■ ■ ■ ■ ■ ■ ■ ■ ■ ■ ■ ■ ■ ■ ■ ■ ■ ■ ■ ■ ■ ■

Groombridge Place Gardens

# LOTS N' LOTS
# OF
# HELPFUL
# INFORMATION

# • GARDEN DESCRIPTIONS •

## 1. JANE AUSTEN'S HOUSE
• 1 mile southwest of Alton, A31, signposted Chawton

A pleasant 'city' garden and the 17th century house where Ms. Austen wrote or revised her six great novels.

## 2. BATEMAN'S (N.T.)
• half mile south of Burwash off A265

This 10 acre garden located in one of Sussex's most beautiful valleys was the home of Rudyard Kipling from 1902 to 1936. Much of the garden was created by Kipling and his wife. There is a series of interesting garden rooms with pear trees forming a pergola, a lovely rose garden, a large lily pond and an extensive herb garden. See Tour 18.

## 3. BEAULIEU
• 6 miles southeast of Lyndhurst on B3056

Quite an attraction, there is something for everyone. If you are in the area you might want to stop and see the Palace House and Gardens, the 13th century Beaulieu Abbey and the National Motor Museum with 250 historic vehicles.

## 4. BORDE HILL GARDENS
• 1.5 miles north of Haywards Heath

Primarily informal woodlands, the rhododendrons and azaleas are brilliant and gorgeous in spring. You will also find beautiful views of the countryside, a nice collection of David Austin roses and many unusual trees and shrubs. See Tour 11.

## 5. BOWOOD HOUSE AND GARDEN
• 1 mile west of Caine on A4

Although this is one of 'Capability' Brown's finest landscapes, many of the most interesting features of this garden are contained in the series of formal terraces around the house. There is a stone fountain with a beautiful nude lounging above, a newly planted partierre and the color from hundreds of roses. From the east terrace there is a breathtaking view of the 40 acre lake and Doric Temple. See Tours 1 and 3.

## 6. BROADLEAS GARDENS
- 1 mile south of Devizes on A360

A small privately owned garden that is best in spring when the rhododendrons are in bloom. The house is accented with blue shutters and doors and the garden with rare blue poppies.

## 7. CHARTWELL (N.T.)
- 2 miles south of Westerham, forking left off B2026

This charming country house and garden with sweeping views over the Weald of Kent was the home of Winston Churchill from 1924 to 1964. Just one of the outstanding features is a beautiful rose garden with yellow and golden colored roses and purple catmint growing below. This was a 50th Anniversary gift to the Churchills from their children. In addition to the lovely garden and wonderful views, you will find an outstanding collection of Churchill's art work and a great deal of history. See Tours 13 and 14.

## 8. CLANDON PARK (N.T.)
- 3 miles east of Guildford, at West Clandon on A247

Eighteenth century Palladian house set amid a classic parkland.

## 9. CLAREMONT LANDSCAPE GARDEN (N.T.)
- south edge of Esher, east side of A307

One of the earliest surviving English landscape gardens, Claremont was touched by the great designers of the time including Vanbrugh, Bridgeman, Kent and Brown. Historically significant. See Tour 9.

## 10. COMPTON ACRES GARDENS
- Canford Cliffs Road in Poole

This is a good place to develop ideas for your own garden. Originally created in 1914, this garden was restored by J.S. Beard after he purchased it in 1950. You will find a glorious Italianesque water garden and a completely authentic Japanese garden among the series of enclosed outdoor rooms. See Tour 4.

## 11. THE COURTS (N.T.)

- 2.5 miles east of Bradford-on-Avon, south side of B3107 in centre of Holt

The design of this 7 acre enclosed garden was influenced by Gertrude Jekyll and Lawrence Johnston. In a series of garden rooms you will find blue and yellow borders, yew hedges, 'bumpy' topiaries, a lily pond and a pillar garden draped with white roses. Much to remind me of my own garden. See Tour 3.

## 12. EMMETTS GARDEN (N.T.)

- 1.5 miles north of Ide Hill off B2042

This charming hillside garden boasts the highest tree top in Kent and naturally has some magnificent views. It was planted at the end of 19th Century in the informal style of Victorian gardener William Robinson.

## 13. EXBURY GARDENS

- 2 miles south of Dibden Purlieu turn south off B3054

The creation of Lionel de Rothschild, this 200 acre woodland garden contains over 1 million rhododendrons and azaleas. Many plants were collected from the Himalayas and China by plant hunters but over 1000 new hybrids have been bred here in the last 80 years. Unbelievable beauty and color from April through early June. See Tour 6.

## 14. FURZEY GARDENS

- 2 miles north of Lyndhurst on a337, turn west to Minstead

Thatched roofs and eight acres of informal gardens filled with rhododendrons, azaleas and a terrific collection of heaths and heathers, that's what you will find here. Early spring is a riot of color from thousands of bulbs and autumn is vibrant with the colors of red, yellow and orange. See Tour 6.

## 15. GOODNESTONE PARK GARDENS

- south of Canterbury off B2046

Enjoy a walk through the Woodland Garden filled with lovely rhododendrons, azaleas. Your patience will be rewarded when you come to the fabulous walled garden. Here you will find a 15th century church that provides a beautiful backdrop for the thriving kitchen garden and borders brimming with color from a superb collection of roses and herbaceous plants. See Tour 10.

**16. GREAT COMP**
- 2 miles east of Borough Green, B2016 off A20

This informal garden, created in the late 20th century, surrounds a 17th century house. You will find mature lime trees and 3000 different plants including a plantsman's collection of trees, shrubs, heathers and herbaceous plants. See Tour 13.

**17. GREAT DIXTER**
- half mile north of Northiam off A28

This gem of the Arts & Crafts Movement is the creation of Edwin Lutyens and more recently plantsman and author, Christopher Lloyd. The famous Long Border is a wonderful mixture of colorful perennials and roses. There is a fine kitchen garden, several beds planted for their contrasts in foliage, a lovely sunken garden and many topiaries including several big, old squirrels. Definitely 'free-spirited'. See Tour 16.

**18. GREATHAM MILL GARDEN**
- 7 miles from Alton on B3006

In this English cottage garden you will find colorful planting beds, the old mill stream filled with bog plants and a Harry Loder's Walking Stick tree that is 15 feet tall.

**19. GROOMBRIDGE PLACE GARDENS**
- 4 miles southwest of Tunbridge Wells on B2110

Arthur Conan Doyle was a frequent visitor to this 17th century moated mansion and garden. Built in a series of garden rooms with yew hedges and brick walls, this gem is a good example of a 17th century walled garden. Restoration of the planting has been done over the last few years but you will find 100 year old Japanese maples in the Oriental garden. See Tour 12.

**20. HATCHLANDS PARK (N.T.)**
- near East Clandon off A246

Here you will find an 18th century house and park designed by Humphry Repton. The west terrace was recently restored to incorporate a Gertrude Jekyll design.

## 21. HEALE GARDEN
- 4 miles north of Salisbury on Woodford Valley Road between A345 & A360

This is a quintessential English garden located on the River Avon. In a formal layout you will find brick walls and stone steps, a wonderful terraced garden designed by Harold Peto and a thriving walled kitchen garden. A scarlet bridge and authentic tea house highlight the lovely Japanese garden. See Tours 4 and 5.

## 22. HEVER CASTLE
- 3 miles southeast of Edenbridge between Sevenoaks and East Grinstead

When you visit this romantic 15th century moated castle you, will find 30 acres of beautiful formal gardens created by American William Waldorf Aster between 1904 and 1908. There is a four acre Italian garden that provides a terrific backdrop for Aster's collection of Roman & Renaissance sculpture and statuary. The loggia provides a wondeful view of the lovely 35 acre lake. See Tours 16 and 17.

## 23. HIGH BEECHES GARDENS
- 1 mile east of A23 at Handcross

Enchanting woodland and water gardens that are at their best in spring and autumn. You will find winding paths, colorful spring flowers, vibrant fall foliage and the soothing sounds of waterfalls.

## 24. SIR HAROLD HILLIER GARDENS
- 3 miles northeast of Romsey off A31

This is a 166 acre arboretum that has one of the best 20th century collections of hardy trees and shrubs. You will find 42,000 plants including the colors of heathers, rhododendrons and azaleas in spring and oaks and maples in autumn. See Tour 7.

### 25. HINTON AMPNER GARDEN (N.T.)
- 1 mile west of Bramdean on A272

Set in the Hampshire countryside, this garden combines a formal design with lovely informal planting. Enjoy the many vistas while you stroll through the 1930's Sunken Garden, the Lily Pond with a long bed of 'Iceberg' roses and along the fragrant philadelphus walk.Take time to inspect the charming mushroom topiaries. See Tour 7 and 8.

### 26. IFORD MANOR
- 7 miles southwest of Bath on A36

This enchanted and romantic garden was designed by Harold Peto and was his home from 1899 to 1933. You will find Peto's extensive collection of Italian statues and pots throughout this fabulous terraced garden. There are wonderful Cotswold stone walls, terra cotta pots filled with colorful plants, old stone columns and borders filled with climbing wisteria and bright peonies. See Tours 1 and 3.

### 27. IGHTHAM MOTE (N.T.)
- 6 miles east of Sevenoaks off A25

This moated manor house covers 650 years of history. Both the house and garden are currently undergoing one of the largest conservation and reconstruction programs ever undertaken by the National Trust. You will find a return to its old romantic charm in the walled kitchen and cutting garden and colorful flower beds. See Tour 14.

### 28. KNOLL GARDENS
- off B3073 between Wimborne and Ferndown

You will find something for all seasons in this four acre 20th century garden. There is a magnificent dragon sculpture surrounded by a colorful partierre in the Dragon Garden. The soothing sounds of waterfalls and a wonderful display of large foliage plants adorn the Water Garden. Don't forget the herbaceous borders and penstemon walk. See Tour 4.

## 29. LEEDS CASTLE
- near Maidstone

Home of the Kings and Queens of medieval England for 300 years, this beautiful castle is surrounded by lovely gardens and magnificent parklands and contains a traditional maze.

## 30. LEONARDSLEE GARDENS
- 4 miles southwest of Horsham on A281

Panoramic views of the countryside can be enjoyed from the Georgian style house and 80 acres of woodland gardens. There is a fabulous collection of mature camellias, rhododendrons and azaleas. You will enjoy the unusual Rock Garden filled with large boulders and colorful Kurume azaleas and dwarf rhododendrons. See Tour 11.

## 31. MARLE PLACE
- 8 miles southeast of Tonbridge

In this charming 10 acre plantman's garden you will find a combination of hedged "rooms' and tree lined avenues. The planting beds are not only designed for color but for contrasts in foliage size and shape. See Tour 15.

## 32. MERRIMENTS GARDENS
- Hawkhurst Road, Hawkhurst

Here, in this four acre garden, you will find several fabulous mixed borders that were designed for flower color and for foliage contrasts. Hard to believe they were created from bare ground over the last five years. There is also a rustic pergola covered with roses, a touch of Giverney and a series of ponds surrounded by a great collection of bog plants. See Tours 16 and 18.

## 33. MOMPESSON HOUSE (N.T.)
- Cathedral Close, center of Salisbury

A small, charming walled garden filled with herbaceous borders, a wisteria and honeysuckle covered pergola and roses climbing on the brick walls. See Tour 5.

### 34. MOTTISFONT ABBEY GARDEN (N.T.)
* 4.5 miles northwest of Romsey

This internationally known rose garden has 350 varieties displayed within the brick walls of the old kitchen garden. Many early 20th century designers contributed to the 21 acre parkland and garden but in the 1970's the famous rose garden was designed and developed by Graham Stuart Thomas. He also contributed a large portion of his own rose collection. See Tours 5 and 7.

### 35. NYMANS GARDEN (N.T.)
* 4.5 miles south of Crawley

This strong, essentially 20th century garden surrounds the romantic and picturesque ruin of the old manor and contains a collection of plants, shrubs and trees from all over the world. You will find a stone pergola in the sunken garden, 147 varieties of old fashioned roses, mixed borders, unusual crown-shaped yew topiaries and many other lovely features. See Tour 12.

### 36. PASHLEY MANOR GARDENS
* between Ticehurst and A21 on B2099

This is an 18th century formal garden created in the English romantic style. The patio room has red brick walls with climbing roses and vistas to the lake and scenic countryside. A large, thriving kitchen garden has a colorful double sided mixed border. Along the Woodland Walk enjoy the color of native rhododendrons and views of fountains in the lake and the house. See Tour 18.

### 37. PENSHURST PLACE
* 3 miles north of Tunbridge Wells

Here you will find a well preserved medieval manor house dating from 1341. The fabulous garden is designed in a series of 'rooms' divided by a **mile** of yew hedges. There is a stunning ten acre walled garden filled with shrub and tree roses, a 100 yard border of massed peonies and lush double sided herbaceous borders. There is also an unusual theater garden. See Tours 14 and 17.

## 38. THE PINES
- 4.5 miles northeast of Dover: Beach Road in St. Margaret's Bay

This is a 6 acre seaside garden with wonderful views to the white cliffs of Dover. You will find a small lake edged with lush water plants, beds of colorful perennials and a terrific rock garden with soothing waterfalls. See Tour 10.

## 39. POLESDEN LACEY (N.T.)
- 5 miles northwest of Dorking

Enjoy the fine views to the surrounding countryside from this 17 acre garden developed by Captain & Mrs. Greville in the early 20th century. There is a 100 foot double sided peony walk and a walled garden with a 450 foot colorful mixed border. Boxwoods, blue geraniums, lavenders and hundreds of roses highlight the large rose garden. See Tour 9.

## 40. SCOTNEY CASTLE (N.T.)
- 6 miles east of Tunbridge Wells on a21

An excellent example of the picturesque period of landscape gardening, your view of the old castle includes a profusion of rhododendrons and magnificent trees. Climbing plants cover the 14th century moated castle while water lilies fill the moat and water loving plants flourish around the edges. A thoroughly romantic spot. See Tour 15.

## 41. SHEFFIELD PARK GARDENS (N.T.)
- 10 miles north of Lewes on A275

A magnificent 100 acre landscape garden with T-shaped chain of five lakes was originally laid out by 'Capability' Brown. Two lakes were added by Humphry Repton in the 18th century. The garden is a riot of color in the spring from rhododendrons and 100's of bulbs and in the fall from tulip trees, maples and chestnuts.

## 42. SISSINGHURST GARDEN (N.T.)
* 7 miles northwest of Tenterden off A262

One of the great masterpieces of the 20th century, it was designed in a series of rooms by Vita Sackville-West and her husband. The 'rooms' are linked by vistas, walks and hedged paths. One of the most famous of these rooms is the White Garden filled with a variety of white flowers and gray and silver foliage. You will find a walled garden with terrific borders and Vita's huge collection of old fashioned roses. There is so much to see you really need to walk to the top of the tower for the best view. See Tours 15 and 16.

## 43. SNAPE COTTAGE
* southwest of Mere on A303

This is a lovely half acre cottage garden with fine views over the Blackmore Vale. It is also a Bed & Breakfast and a good place to stop in your travels. See Tour 2.

## 44. SPINNERS
* 2 miles north of Lymington off a337

Created over the past 25 years, this is a plantsman's garden that has retained the spirit of the adjacent New Forest. The woodland atmosphere is lush with rhododendrons, azaleas and Japanese maples. Truly a spring garden. See Tour 6.

## 45. SQUERRYES COURT
* half mile west of Westerham off A25

The fifteen acres of historic gardens you will find here were originally laid out in 1709 in a formal Anglo-Dutch style. Although the landscape was changed to a more natural look in the 18th century, the owners are in the process of restoring the 18th century formality and charm. Features that have been restored in the last ten years are an intricate partierre and several mixed borders contained within clipped yew hedges. See Tour 13.

## 46. STANDEN (N.T.)

- 2 miles south of East Grinstead off B2110

This house is an excellent example of the Arts & Crafts Movement and contains original Morris & Co. furnishings. The terraced garden provides fabulous views across the Medway Valley. Lovely in all seasons but spring is the most marvelous time to visit. See Tour 12.

## 47. STOURHEAD (N.T.)

- at Stourton off B3092, 3 miles northwest of Mere

One of the finest landscape gardens of the 18th century, it contains an unbelievable collection of matured trees that were combined to provide this wonderful setting. The path that encircles the lake guides you through a woodland garden of colorful plants and it provides views to several magnificent follies. Included are a marvelous Palladian Bridge, an elegant Pantheon and a grotto with a 'porthole' that looks out to the lake. See Tours 1 and 2.

## 48. STOURTON HOUSE

- 3 miles north of Mere next to Stourhead at A303

You will enjoy this 4 acre English cottage garden. An unusual and impressively shaped hedge is created by the 27 year old Leyland cypress. A riot of color from spring to fall is provided by large beds of delphiniums, a rose covered pergola and borders filled with herbaceous plants. Many of these flowers are collected, dried and sold in bouquets by the lovely lady who owns this garden. See Tour 2.

## 49. UPPARK (N.T.)

- 5 miles southeast of Petersfield on B2146

This house was placed on high ground to provide extraordinary views of rolling hills and pastureland. Although most of Humphry Repton's terraced gardens have disappeared, you will find lovely kidney shaped planting beds filled with bearded irises, daylilies and geraniums. The refurbished house has become quite an attraction. See Tour 8.

## 50. WAKEHURST PLACE GARDEN (N.T.)
- 1.5 miles northwest of Ardingly on B2028

A part of the Royal Botanic Gardens at Kew, this woodland garden is particularly noted for its rare trees and flowering shrubs. The delightful Wetland Garden contains a collection of plants, from cat tails to skunk cabbage, selected for their foliage contrasts. A charming fountain sculpture of a child playing horns highlights the walled garden. See Tour 11.

## 51. WALMER CASTLE
- on coast south of Walmer on A258

Along the Dover coast you will find this 16th century castle which is now the domestic residence of the Queen Mother. The double sided borders are backed by yew hedges clipped in an unusual form, see if you can guess. There is a small rose garden and a nicely maintained colorful kitchen and cutting garden. See Tour 10.

## 52. WEST DEAN GARDENS
- outside town of West Dean

A real find! The present 30 acre garden has undergone many changes since the late 18th century. The most recent contribution was made in the early 20th century by Harold Peto. From the wonderful terraced sunken garden you climb the stone steps up to Peto's fabulous 100 meter long pergola. It is covered with roses, wisteria and clematis and lined with colorful borders. See Tour 8.

## 53. GILBERT WHITE'S HOUSE AND GARDEN
- in village of Selbourne on B3006

This quaint city garden is a work in progress. You will find several lovely features including a colorful walled garden, a laburnum covered pergola and a topiary wall. See Tours 7 and 8.

### 54. WILTON HOUSE
- 3 miles west of Salisbury on a30

Little of the 17th century classical garden remains in this 21 acre parkland. What you will find is a stately Palladian Bridge, a lovely walled rose garden and three colorful planting beds surrounded by water and connected by several bright red oriental style bridges. There is also a whispering bench if you have any secrets to tell. See Tour 5.

### 55. WISLEY GARDEN
- off A3 near Woking

This is the world famous 240 acre garden of the Royal Horticultural Society. There are several wonderful features including a large terraced pond filled with water lilies, an extensive rock garden built up the side of the hill, a herb garden surrounded by a hornbeam hedge and a huge rose garden that is divided into four glorious sections. See Tour 9.

# • BIOGRAPHIES OF GARDENERS •

### Charles Bridgeman (d. 1738)

Most notable works: Claremont, Surrey; Chiswick House, London; Kensington Gardens, London; Rousham House, Oxfordshire; Stowe, Buckinghamshire

* He helped bridge the gap between the formality of the late 17th century and the emerging 'landscape' period.
* His style retained the details and characteristics of formality but was asymmetrical and presented a relationship between the garden and the surrounding countryside.
* A practical gardening knowledge and his professional training as a surveyor which enabled him to cope with large scale designs were his two main assets. He could convert ideas onto paper and then into reality.
* He was a pupil of George London & Henry Wise, the leading gardening partnership during the reign of William & Mary.
* In 1728 he succeeded Wise as the royal gardener and retained that position until his death.
* Much of his work was altered or destroyed by 'Capability' Brown and others during the 'Landscape Movement'.
* He worked on Stowe & Claremont with Sir John Vanbrugh and was greatly influenced by his style. Bridgeman continued to work at Stowe from 1715 until shortly before his death in 1738.
* Although Rousham Park is acknowledged as William Kent's most outstanding work, he did work closely within the framework of Bridgeman's original layout. Some of Bridgeman's features still remain such as the 'natural theater' and the bowling green lawn.
* He is considered by many to be the first to use the 'ha-ha' in England.

### Lancelot "Capability" Brown- 1716-1783

Most notable works: too numerous to list them all but those included in this book are Bowood House, Wiltshire; Blenheim Palace, Oxfordshire; Stowe, Buckinghamshire; Warwick Castle, Warwickshire

* Even after 200 years, Brown's stamp on the English countryside remains unmistakable. His work was so close to nature that, since the landscapes have now reached maturity, it is indistinguishable.

Brown (continued)
- He did destroy many lovely gardens but he did create many fine landscapes and established a garden style that belonged to Britain alone.
- During his 40 year career he refined the concept of landscape so that it became dependent on three simple factors: trees, water, terrain.
- His ideal landscape had gentle contours, water and a minimum of man-made interruptions. To achieve his goal he planted thousands of native trees, moved huge qualities of earth and damned streams to create lakes.
- Brown took the job as head gardener at Stowe when he was in his twenties. He learned from the work of William Kent and eventually contributed to the last two major phases of Stowe's development.
- By the time Brown left Stowe (after 9 years), he had already completed several commissions and had established himself as the leading landscape designer of the day.
- In his redesign of Warwick Castle, he removed the small formal gardens and replaced them with lawn.
- He was appointed surveyor to His Majesty's gardens and waters at Hampton Court in 1764.

**William Sawrey Gilpin (1762-1843)**
Most notable works: Scotney Castle, Kent; Nuneham Park, Oxfordshire
- Gilpin was the last major advocate of the 'picturesque movement' before it became absorbed by the Victorian era.
- At Scotney Castle he created one of the most acclaimed landscapes of the 'pictuesque movement'. On his advice the new house was built on top of the hill looking down on the castle ruins.
- In 1832 he published *Practical Hints for Landscape Gardeners*.

**Sir Geoffrey Jellicoe (1900- 1996)**
Most notable works: Ditchley Park, Oxfordshire; Royal Lodge, Berkshire; Sutton Place, Surrey; Pusey, Oxfordshire
- He is generally acknowledged as one of the foremost British garden and landscape designer of the 20th century.

**Jellicoe (continued)**
- He had the ability to reconcile the traditions of the past with contemporary ideas. In his early years he combined his admiration for Italian Renaissance gardens with a strong commitment to modernism as demonstrated at Ditchley Park.

**Gertrude Jekyll (1843-1932)**

Most notable works: too numerous to list but a few examples are Barrington Court, Somerset; Hestercombe, Somerset; Lambay Castle, Eire; Marsh Court, Hampshire; Munstead Wood, Surry; Woodside, Buckinghamshire

- Jekyll made an unequaled contribution to the foundation of gardens as we know them today. She demonstrated how gardening could best be scaled down in a modest home without sacrificing on quality or interest.
- She helped to bridge the gap between professional and amateur gardeners and promoted the involvement of women.
- A simple portrait of Jekyll indicates she was trained as a painter and worked as a craftswoman. She had an encyclopedic memory of both wild and cultivated plants and a fondness for the simple life.
- Preferring the small and intimate to the large and expansive, she paid attention to detail in plant color, in form and in architectural materials.
- A friendship and working relationship developed between Jekyll and Edwin Lutyens. The most fruitful years of their partnership were 1897 to 1908.
- Certain guidelines and techniques were constants in all Jekyll and Lutyen's work together: 1) unity between house and garden, 2) between planting and architectural features, 3) between various areas of the garden.
- Unfortunately, little of her work remains in its original form.
- She began her writing career in the 1870's with magazine articles in *The Garden* and she wrote her first book in 1899.

**Major Lawrence Johnston (1871-1958)**

Most notable work: Hidcote Manor, Gloucestershire
- Johnston was an American, who was born in Paris, educated in England and became a naturalized British citizen in 1900.

Johnston (continued)

- The farm at Hidcote was purchased for him by his mother on his return from the war in South Africa.
- He had no practical experience or professional training but he did have a clear idea of how the garden should evolve.
- Johnston was able to indulge his acquired skills and knowledge of plants in all the different planting beds he created. He enclosed those beds with a variety of hedges including hollies, yews, beeches and hornbeams.
- He joined two plant collecting expeditions between 1907 and 1914, the first to southern Africa, the second to Yunnan in China.

## William Kent (1685-1748)

Most notable works: Claremont, Surrey; Chiswick House, London; Rousham House, Oxfordshire; Stowe, Buckinghamshire

- He initiated the change known as the 'landscape' movemen at the beginning of the 18th century.
- Horace Walpole called him "The father of modern gardening. He leapt the fence and saw that all nature was a garden." The influence of Kent's garden designs was enormous through the balance of the 18th century and beyond.
- Although we consider him a painter, landscape gardener and architect, he was more architect as seen from the structures (temples, obelisks, gateways) he put into his plans.
- He had a more visual approach to design. There is no evidence that he drew up plans or wrote down his ideas (except in letters) which allowed him to create with a greater freshness.
- Kent spent nine years in Italy starting in his late twenties. The architecture, paintings and gardens he studied there were a great inspiration to him throughout his career.
- Probably the most significant influence to his career as a landscape architect was Alexander Pope who believed that "all gardening is landscape painting".
- He added his own ideas to the designs of Bridgeman at Stowe, Rousham and Claremont. Rousham is considered Kent's masterpiece.

### Norah Lindsay (1866-1948)

Most notable works: Mottisfont Abbey, Hampshire; Godmersham Park, Kent; Port Lympne, Kent

- Lindsay has been described as "one of the first amateur-professional garden designers who did so much to uphold the renown of English gardens during the years immediately preceding and succeeding World War I."
- She was significantly influenced by the gardens of Florence and Rome.
- Her forte was the association of herbaceous plants in the much loved English borders.
- The charming knot garden at Mottisfont Abbey was her creation.

### Christopher Lloyd (1921-)

Most notable work: Great Dixter, Sussex

- Lloyd, a well known 'amateur' gardener, whose influence is based on his gardening skill and his independent views on garden design and planting.
- He put his views and originality into practice at Great Dixter, the Lloyd family home.
- His principles of planting, plant association and use of unusual plants have been put to use in many areas of Great Dexter but none more than his wonderful Long Border.
- The pioneer of mixed borders, Lloyd's first book *The Mixed Border* written in 1957 promotes the concept that all kinds of plants should be 'encouraged to cohabit'.
- He wrote many authoritative books from 1965 to 1984. His most influential book, *The Well-Tempered Garden* written in 1970, gives a comprehensive view and practice of his style of gardening.

### George London (d. 1713)

Most notable works: Hampton Court, London; Blenheim Palace, Oxfordshire; Melbourne Hall, Derbyshire; Hanbury Hall, Hereford & Worcester

- In 1681 London established Brompton Nurseries, the first English commercial nursery. He was joined by Henry Wise in 1687.

London (continued)

- The partnership of London & Wise was the foremost designer of formal gardens during the reigns of William & Mary and Queen Anne.
- Influences from Italy and France were incorporated into the English landscape.
- The formality of the hedges and the intricate patterns of gardens beds they created at places like Blenheim Palace caused some of the strongest reactions from members of the landscape movement.
- Unfortunately much of their work disappeared in the face of that more naturalistic style of the 18th century.

### Sir Edwin Lutyens (1869-1944)

Most notable works: too numerous to provide a total list but a few examples are Great Dexter, Sussex; Long Barn, Kent; Munstead Wood, Surrey

- One of the most original and sought-after architects of his time.
- He met Gertrude Jekyll when he was just 20 and his education as an architect was influenced in such a manner to set him apart from his contemporaries.
- His partnership with Jekyll created a wonderful harmony between house and garden, a place to live in, a place to enjoy. The balance they sought formed a cornerstone for 20th century gardens.
- In later years Lutyens developed a more individual and classical style demonstrated in the grand formal canal gardens he created after World War I.
- His garden architecture stressed the importance of strong directional lines and horizontal and vertical surfaces again demonstrated in his strong hedges.
- He created some of the best known garden furniture designs of the early 20th century.

### William Morris (1834-1896)

- Morris was a designer and decorator, a creator of wonderful textiles, a poet and political activist and the 'creator' of the Arts & Crafts Movement of the 19th Century.
- He rebelled against the Victorian period and his own privileged upbringing and grew to believe in the simplicities of life.

- His concept of the ideal home was: "Have nothing in your houses that you do not know to be useful, or believe to be beautiful."
- In 1861 he set up the Morris & Co. firm, a decorating company that provided not only decorating services but products such as fabrics and wallpapers.

## Harold Peto (1854-1933)

Most notable works: Heale House, Wiltshire; Iford Manor, Wiltshire; West Dean, West Sussex; Buscot Park, Oxfordshire

- Peto had an architects eye and a true feel for the use of plants.
- He had a great admiration for the delights of Renaissance Italy and a growing interest in the relationship between house and garden.
- In 1876 he established an architectural partnership with Ernest George. It became one of the most respected practices of the late Victorian and Edwardian periods.
- In 1886 Edwin Lutyens was taken on as a pupil.
- Peto set up his own firm in 1892 and offered garden design and garden architecture.
- At his home, Iford Manor, he was able to study garden design and garden development over several years.

## Humphry Repton (1752-1818)

Most notable works: too numerous to list but a few examples are Uppark, Sussex; Hatchlands, Surrey; Sezincote, Gloucestershire

- 'Capability' Brown's successor, he adapted the "landscape movement" to the emerging prosperous middle class. He added "practicality" to Kent and Brown's ideas.
- In 1788, in his late 30's, with little formal training, he turned from architecture to garden design out of financial necessity. In a very short time he had a busy and successful career with recommendations from many satisfied clients.
- For Repton four requisites were needed for a perfect landscape design: 1)design must hide natural defects and display natural beauties, 2)boundaries should be carefully hidden or disguised, 3)the look should be natural, 4)objects of convenience or comfort must be removed or concealed if it isn't possible to

Repton (continued)

- He sited houses near the buildings (barns, stables, etc.) that serviced the household and he felt that the style of the house should be closely reflected in the style of its surroundings.
- He had a feeling for the use of plants and a knowledge of their appropriateness to compliment various architectural styles.
- He reintroduced the terrace and, to a certain extent, flowers to the garden.
- A 'Red Book' system for presenting proposals to each client was created.
- Like so many others, much of his work has either disappeared or been seriously altered.

## William Robinson (1838-1935)

Most notable works: Nymans Gardens, Sussex; Gravetye Manor, Sussex

- Robinson had a dramatic influence on the development of gardens through his writing. He advocated a more natural style as opposed to the formal Victorian style.
- Gertrude Jekyll was unstinting in her admiration and was obviously influenced by him while Edwin Lutyens thought of him as a "foozle-headed old bore".
- He took a job at the Royal Botanic Garden in Regent's Park in 1861 where his particular domain was the collection of hardy herbaceous plants.
- His writing career began in 1866. In his third book, *Alpine Flowers for English Gardens* in 1870, he began to put into words his ideas for improvements to English gardens.
- In 1871 he founded the weekly publication *The Garden*, which was a regular outlet for his ideas.
- In 1883 he collected all his material into *The English Flower Garden,,* the cornerstone of his reputation.
- He bought the property at Gravetye Manor in 1885, where he mixed his own ideas on garden design with some formal features such as terracing, pergolas and trellis.
- Evidence of his influence can be found in gardens all over the country.

## The Hon Victoria Mary"Vita" Sackville-West (1892-1962)

Most notable works: Sissinghurst Castle, Kent; Long Barn, Kent
- Sissinghurst, considered the quintessential English garden of the 20th Century, is the personal creation of Sackville-West and her husband, Harold Nicolson. It became a model for the contemporary garden.
- Long Barn, purchased by the couple in 1915, was their first creation.
- She preferred to be known as a writer than as a gardener and as a poet and biographer she achieved notable distinction.
- From 1947 to 1961, she wrote a weekly column on gardening in the *Observer* .

### Graham Stuart Thomas (1909-)

Most notable works: Mottisfont Abbey, Hampshire; Sezincote, Gloucestershire
- Thomas has been the champion of old fashioned shrub roses and has been largely responsible for their return to popularity.
- He is a plantsman, designer, painter, historian and journalist who studied horticulture at Cambridge University Botanic Garden.
- As garden adviser for the National Trust from 1955 to 1974, he masterminded a number of outstanding garden restorations such as: Claremont Landscape Garden and Westbury Court.
- In 1972 he designed a rose garden for the National Trust at Mottisfont Abbey. The collection of old fashioned roses that he began to build after the war provided the nucleus for this internationally famous garden.
- He has written a series of books on roses, including *The Old Shrub Roses (1995)* which remains his most popular. He has also written books on perennials and ground covers among others.

### Sir John Vanbrugh (1664-1726)

Most notable works: Claremont, Surrey; Queen's Theatre, London; Blenheim Palace, Oxfordshire; Stowe, Buckinghamshire

■■■■■■■■■■■■■■■■■■■■■■■■■■■■■■■■■■■■■■■■■

### Vanbrugh (continued)

- Vanbrugh was a soldier, a playwrite and, finally, an architect.
- He developed a style of baroque architecture that was unique in England.
- The idea that gardens, like painted landscapes, are composed of lakes, temples, woods and vistas was first conceived by Vanbrugh.
- He was committed to a strongly structured, balanced, geometric plan.
- He worked with Charles Bridgeman on Claremont and Stowe. Unfortunately, out of all the garden buildings he designed at Stowe only the rotunda still survives.

### Rosemary Verey (1918-)

Most notable works: Barnsley House, Gloucestershire
- One of the best known contemporary garden authorities in England. Mrs. Verey exemplifies the manor in which 'amateur' gardeners and garden writers have influenced today's garden.
- The foundations of her garden work are a fascination with garden history and a love of plants.
- She has had great success incorporating period features from Tudor and 17th century gardens into a modern design.
- Since 1980 she has written several books on garden design and style.
- Barnsley House, her best known work and her home, has provided much of the research and material for her books.

■■■■■■■■■■■■■■■■■■■■■■■■■■■■■■■■■■■■■■■

# • GARDEN DESIGN PERIODS •

## FORMAL GARDEN DESIGN

In the 16th Century the pleasure garden began to appear. Instead of being a place to just look at, it became a place to spend time in, to entertain in and to enjoy. The garden layout or design was rigid, symetrical and formal with knots, hedges and colorful flowers. There were tennis courts, bowling greens and imitation animals.

In the 17th Century, design was influenced by the Renaissance. Many of the garden designers of this period were French, i.e.: the Huguenot Brothers and Isaac de Caus. The concept was that the house and garden should compliment each other. Most of the grand gardens of the pre-Civil War period were enclosed by walls and there was little connection with the surrounding landscape.

An increasing interest in the horticultural side of gardening developed during this time. This was demonstrated by the creation of the Oxford Botanical Garden in 1621 and the success of plant collectors such as John Tradescant and his son John who traveled not only to the continent but to the New World.

The Jacobeans and the Stuarts brought gardening to a fine art. One's garden became a reflection of one's status. Fountains and water features were used and topiaries became popular once again.

During the Restoration, in the later half of the 17th Century, the aristocracy brought back ideas from their travels in Europe and the French style was at its height. Smaller landowners began to take an interest in gardening. There was an increasing importance placed in the relationship between garden and surrounding countryside even during this period. This was to lay some of the foundation for the "landscape movement".

It was obvious that the New World had a wealth of horticultural treasures. The most extensive collection of North American trees and shrubs in England was acquired by Henry Compton

Formal Design (continued)

for his garden at Fulham Palace. Compton, an influential figure in the plant trade, employed George London as gardener for several years starting in 1681.

The Dutch influence was also very popular. Their designs were geometric in their formality but smaller in scale than the French. The Dutch had also established themselves as plantsmen without equal and they displayed a true enjoyment in flower gardening.

Even with all these influences from Europe and America, England retained a clear measure of independence. Although much of what was created during this period was dramatically changed or even destroyed during the "Landscape Movement", the groundwork for England's future influence in the gardening field was established.

A few of the gardeners of the period were Charles Bridgeman, William Kent, George London and Henry Wise and Sir John Vanbrugh.

## "LANDSCAPE MOVEMENT"- THE NATURAL LOOK

The Landscape Movement began in the early 18th Century and coincided with the Georgian period of architecture. It was a reaction to the formality and contrivances of the 17th century (topiaries, knot gardens, parterres) and a social reaction to the monarchy in favor of the landed gentry.

A respect for nature, "an essential factor of human life", became part of the philosophy of the time. It was felt that gardens should take their inspiration from nature. The garden became part of the countryside and the countryside came into the garden. Geometrical symmetry was replaced by asymmetry and serpentine curves.

Craftsmanship was also a part of the movement; wrought iron work was transformed into decorative gates and arbors and there were finely worked lead statues and urns.

The second half of the 18th Century was clearly dominated by Lancelot "Capability" Brown who carried the movement to an extreme. He created hundreds of acres of landscape parks. Hundreds of tons of dirt were moved to create a "natural" look, rivers were diverted or dammed and hills were built or removed. Hedges, parterres and flowers were removed, walls and fences were replaced by ha-has and architectural monuments became an integral part of the landscape.

Although horticulture took a backseat during this period, there was a continuing exchange of plant materials and ideas between England and the United States. The first varieties of rhododendrons and several ornamental trees and shrubs were imported from North America.

In the later part of the 18th Century, the "picturesque" movement developed. The preference was for a landscape of the natural scenery of mountains, streams and woodlands. This was again a reaction, but this time to Brown and his artificial landscapes.

Near the turn of the century Humphry Repton, who had initially followed in Brown's footsteps, was responsible for a transitional period when ornamental flower gardens and terraces were reintroduced into the "landscape".

A few of the gardeners of the period from England and the United States were Lancelot "Capability" Brown, Thomas Jefferson, Humphry Repton, George Washington.

## VICTORIAN PERIOD

This was the real beginning of the English passion for gardening. The formal garden of the 17th century was reinstated. Huge and elaborate gardens were designed to compliment the flamboyant mansions of the period. Small cottage gardens became popular with the more prosperous middle class and even the working class had their window boxes.

The industrial revolution played a part in the new garden design. Coal furnaces heated greenhouses and the brick walls

Victorian Period (continued)

of kitchen gardens. Steam engines provided the power for garden fountains. The removal of the glass tax in 1845 opened the door to the building of conservatories and greenhouses. In addition, the wealth accumulated from industrial and commercial enterprises provided the money to create the great houses and gardens of this period.

The plant trade continued to grow. David Douglas introduced conifers from the United States, rhododendrons were introduced from the Himalayas and the fashionable scented-leafed geraniums were imported from South Africa.

This was the start of new gardening magazines and books, new kinds of garden tools and the first lawn mower which was invented in 1830.

Lawn was an essential element (made easier by the mower), roses were an important part of all the big estates and rock gardens were all the rage.

Americans greatly admired the public parks and gardens of the Victorian Period. F.L. Olmsted, an American landscape architect, visited England in 1850. His designs for parks such as Central Park in New York were greatly influenced by what he saw during his visit.

The Victorian influence remains in England today through the public parks and the colorful window boxes, hanging baskets and pots of geraniums, lobelia and aubretia seen throughout the country.

A few of the gardeners of the period were Humphry Repton, James Bateman, Robert Holford, Frederick Law Olmsted.

## ARTS & CRAFTS MOVEMENT

In the last part of the 19th century in England, the Arts & Crafts Movement developed as a reaction to the ostentations of the Victorian period. It was a desire to emphasize craftsmanship, the qualities of the rural life and a more natural style.

At the center of the movement was designer William Morris who formed William Morris & Co. in 1861 with the goal of revitalizing the arts through craftsmanship. Morris, who was very fond of the Cotswolds, encouraged his friends to move there and a large number of craftsmen did move to Chipping Camden at the turn of the century

Munstead Wood in Surrey, designed by Edwin Lutyens for Gertrude Jekyll, is a good example of the movement. It incorporated Bargate stone walls, hand made tiles and mullion windows. Another example is Great Dixter which was designed by Christopher Lloyd.

## EARLY 20th CENTURY

The garden once again became social, a place for activity. It was no longer a place to merely be looked upon from the house but was something to be lived in, a continuation of the house with outdoor rooms.

The reaction to the Victorian garden took many forms. One was informal, a return to the natural look (the A & C Movement); another was formal in the overall look of the architecture and the garden. The third form provided a balance between architecture and horticulture, had an attention to details and could be adapted to any scale.

The biggest advocate for informality and more natural planting was William Robinson. Although a gardener in his own right, he was primarily a writer who had much influence on the designs of the day and on the future work of people like Gertrude Jekyll.

The model for the more formal gardens was the Italian Renaissance. Harold Peto and the water garden he designed at Buscot Park and Achille Duchene's water terrace at Blenheim Palace are good examples of this style.

The most lasting garden style was established by Gertrude Jekyll & Edwin Lutyens. Their gardens did not require expansive acreage and settings to achieve the desired affect and they demonstrated that the garden could have several looks

Early 20th Century (continued)

throughout the year. They focused on regional architecture, local materials and placed a strong emphasis on plantsmanship. Future generations of designers and gardeners in England and America have followed their example and guidelines.

A few of the gardeners of the period were Gertrude Jekyll, Edwin Lutyens, Lawrence Johnston, Harold Peto, William Robinson, Achille Duchene.

## MID 20th CENTURY

In the post World War I period, people did more of the gardening themselves. They looked for designs that were more understated and displayed planting rather than architectural monuments.

In the United States, Frank Lloyd Wright developed the "Prairie School" of architecture. During that same time Jans Jensen's garden designs became known as the "prairie style". An important part of his designs was his use of trees and plants that were native to a particular area.

In England a desire for informality was expressed in the creation of natural woodland gardens. Native trees, flowering and ornamental trees and shrubs and spring bulbs extended a garden's life throughout most of the year. The garden at the Rothschild estate, Exbury, was created during this period. Begun in 1919, it is over 200 acres of woodlands with a remarkable collection of rhododendrons and azaleas.

For most people, however, the typical 20th Century garden did not require hundreds of acres or famous designers. The style was 'compartments', outdoor rooms with walls or hedges created out of hollies, yews or hornbeams as Lawrence Johnston did at Hidcote and 'Vita' Sackville-West did at Sissinghurst. The look was colorful borders with roses and perennials.

A few of the gardeners of the period were Lawrence Johnston, 'Vita' Sackville-West, Thomas Church, Jans Jensen.

## LATE 20th CENTURY

These are the days of the gifted "amateur" gardeners such as Penelope Hobhouse (one of my favorites), Christopher Lloyd and Rosemary Verey who, through their own gardens and their books and lectures, have reached a wider audience than many "professionals".

Garden styles have been borrowed from the past and mixed together with great freedom to create individual design and charm.

A few of the gardeners of the period are Penelope Hobhouse, Geoffrey Jellicoe, Christopher Lloyd, Rosemary Verey.

# • GLOSSARY OF TERMS •

**Allee-** a formal hedged walk or road within the "wilderness".

**Avenue-** formed by successive pairs of trees or other identical shapes (pots or statues) flanking a drive, walk or pathway; gives a linear perspective and an impression of distance. See the grand avenue of lime trees at Goodnestone Park.

**Belvedere-** summerhouse on a high or lofty place, such as a hill, in a garden. You will find a medieval-style belvedere at Claremont Landscape Garden.

**Bog Garden-** a marshy area with plants that love wet feet and need permanently saturated soil and almost no drainage. Visit the Wetland Garden at Wakehurst Place.

**Cottage Garden-** a grand and colorful mixture of hollyhocks, sunflowers, pansies and roses, fruits, vegetables and lots of herbs. The garden beds, dating back to the 14th Century, overflow paths leading to the front of small country homes and are often duplicated as herbaceous borders in large estates and in suburban homes. Many of Gertrude Jekyll's ideas for borders were influenced by the cottage themes.

**Dovecote-** a small building, raised above the ground, in which pigeons nest. Don't miss the thatched roof dovecote at Heale Garden.

**Espalier-** a tree or row of trees (usually fruit) trained to grow flat on a latticework or trellis. See the kitchen garden at Heale Garden and the nut trees at Penshurst Place.

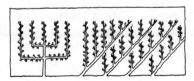

**Folly-** a building, often in the shape of a ruin, set in a garden or landscape purely for fun. See the many lovely follies at Stourhead.

**Grotto**- a hidden underground passage, an ornamental cave; usually containing a water feature. Remember to look for the fabulous grotto at Stourhead.

**Ha-Ha**- a nearly invisible sunken barrier shaped like a ditch or dry moat, used instead of a raised barrier, wall or hedge to keep cattle out of the garden. It gives the illusion the garden and the surrounding countryside are one. See if you can spot the one at Bowood or Mottisfont Abbey.

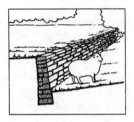

**Herbaceous Border**- beds of hardy perennials, many grown for cut flowers, originally planted to bloom for a short time in the summer but the new "mixed" border blooms from early spring until late fall; roses and peonies are often included. You will find these in every garden, after all it wouldn't be England without it, but some of the best are at Goodnestone Park, Sissinghurst and Merriments.

**Knots**- a pattern of intersecting bands of different herbs or low hedged planting beds; there are many examples in these tours, but one of the nicest is at Groombridge Place.

**Loggia**- an arched or roofed gallery projecting from the side of a building. Look for an wonderful fountain in the loggia at Hever Castle and Iford Manor's arched loggia.

**Maze**- a layout in which hedges are used to mark out a confusing pattern; the best known maze in England, planted in 1690, is in Hampton Court. See the 80 foot square maze at Hever Castle.

**Oast House**- hops, one of the major ingredients in beer making, are dried in these buildings. Seen all over Kent, there are good examples at Great Dixter and Sissinghurst.

**Obelisks**- a tall, slender four sided pillar, gradually tapering as it rises, having the top in the form of a pyramid. One of these unusual monuments is featured at Stourhead.

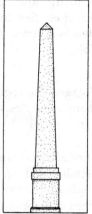

**Orangery**- orange trees were prized by English gardeners above almost any fruit and the orangery (or conservatory or greenhouse) was built to protect them and other tender plants from the winter cold.

**Parterre**- the ornamental garden close to the palace or house, composed of low patterns in boxwood, grass or flowers; it was invented in the 16th century for the Queen of France. There are parterres in many gardens but the simple flower beds at Knoll Gardens.

**Pergola**- a series of constructed arches that create a pathway and can be decorative or covered with climbing and twining plants. The Harold Peto design at West Dean is fabulous.

**Pleaching-** technique used for training and shaping trees into architectural forms they would not naturally take, done by bending and intertwining branches. See the wonderful pleached limes at Mottisfont Abbey.

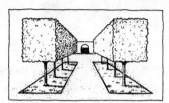

**Potager-** the vegetable or kitchen garden. There are certainly many examples, the large thriving garden at Pashley Manor is very special.

**Rondel-** circular grassy areas surrounded by a hedge (Kentish people used term, an area used to dry hops). The lawned areas at Sissinghurst are best seem from the Tower.

**Topiary-** clipped evergreens, some in elaborate forms, some in simple cones or pyramids. They came into their own in the 17th Century and were the first to go in the landscape movement. There are unusual crown shapes at Nymans and fun shapes like squirrels at Great Dixter, mushrooms at Hinton Ampner and turtles at Nymans.

**Vista-** artificially created view of the countryside usually created by planting an avenue of trees.

# • GARDEN PARTICULARS •

| # | GARDEN NAME | CITY | PHONE NUMBER | NATIONAL TRUST | MONTHS OPEN | DAYS OPEN | HOURS OPEN | FEE/ AMOUNT | FOOD SERVICE | PICNIC AREA | REST ROOM | GIFT SHOP |
|---|---|---|---|---|---|---|---|---|---|---|---|---|
| •1 | Jane Austen's House | Alton | 01420 83262 | No | Apr-Oct | Daily | 11:00-4:30 | £2.00,chd50p | No | No | No | No |
| 2 | Bateman's | Burwash | (01435) 882302 | Yes | Apr thru Oct | Daily exThu&Fri | 11:00-5:30 | £4.50,chd£2.25 | Yes | No | Yes | Yes |
| •3 | Beaulieu | Beaulieu | (01590) 612345 | No | Apr-Oct | Daily | 10:00-6:00 | £6.75,chd£4.50 | Yes | Yes | Yes | Yes |
| 4 | Borde Hill | Haywards Heath | 01444 450326 | No | midMar-Oct | Daily | 10:00-6:00 | £2.00,chd£1.00 | Yes | Yes | Yes | No |
| 5 | Bowood Rhododendron Walk / Bowood House & Garden | Caine | 01249 812102 | No | Apr thru Oct | Daily / Daily | 11:00-6:00 / 11:00-6:00 | £5.00,chd£2.80 | Yes | Yes | Yes | Yes |
| •6 | Broadleas Gardens | Salisbury | 01380 722035 | No | Apr toOct | Sun,Wed,Thur | 2:00-6:00 | £2.50,chd£1.00 | Yes, Sun | No | Yes | Yes |
| 7 | Chartwell | Westerham | (0732) 866368 | Yes | Apr thru Oct | Daily exMon & Fri | 11:00-5:30 | £4.50,chd£2.25 | Yes | No | Yes | Yes |
| •8 | Clandon Park | West Clandon | (0483) 222482 | Yes | Apr thru Oct | Sat-Wed | 1:30-5:30 | £4.00,chd£2.00 | Yes | No | Yes | Yes |
| 9 | Claremont Landscape Garden | Esher | (0372) 469421 | Yes | Apr thru Oct | Mon-Fri / Sat,Sun,Bk Hol Mon | 10:00-6:00 / 10:00-7:00 | £3.00 | Yes | No | Yes | Yes |
| 10 | Compton Acres | Poole | 01202 700778 | Yes | Mar thru Oct | Daily | 10:00-6:00 | £4.50,chd£1.00 | Yes | No | Yes | No |
| 11 | Courts, The | Holt | (0225) 782340 | Yes | Apr thru Oct | Daily ex Sat | 2:00-5:00 | £2.80,chd£1.40 | No | No | No | No |
| •12 | Emmetts Garden | Sevenoaks | 01732 750367 | Yes | Apr thru Oct | Wed,Sat,Sun, Bk Hol Mon | 11:00-5:30 | £3.00,chd£150 | Yes | Yes | Yes | No |
| 13 | Exbury Gardens | Southampton | 01703 891203 | No | Mar thru Oct | Daily | 10:00-5:30 | £4.80,chd£3.80 | Yes | Yes | Yes | Yes |
| 14 | Furzey Gardens | Minstead | 01703 812464 | No | All | Daily | 10:00-5:00 | £3.00,chd£1.50 | Yes | Yes | Yes | Yes |
| 15 | Goodnestone Park Gardens | Wingham | 01304 840107 | No | Apr thru Oct | Mon,Wed,Thu,Fri / Sun | 11:00-5:00 / 12:00-6:00 | £2.50,chd20p | Occas. | No | No | No |
| 16 | Great Comp | Sevenoaks | 01732 886154 | No | Mar thru Oct | Daily | 11:00-6:00 | £3.00,chd£1.00 | Yes | No | Yes | No |
| 17 | Great Dixter | Northiam | 01797 252878 | No | Apr-midOct | Tue-Sun,Bk Hol Mon | 2:00-5:00 | £4.00,chd50p | No | No | Yes | No |
| •18 | Greatham Mill Garden | Greatham | 01420 538245 | No | Feb thru Sep | Daily | 2:00-6:00 | £2.00 | Yes,wknds | No | Yes | No |
| 19 | Groombridge Place Gardens | Tunbridge wells | 01892 863999 | No | Apr thru Oct | Daily | 10:00-6:00 | £5.00,chd£3.50 | Yes | No | Yes | Yes |
| •20 | Hatchlands Park | East Clandon | (0483) 222787 | Yes | Apr thru Oct | Tue,Wed,Thu,Sun,Bk Hol Mon | 2:00-5:30 | £4.00,chd£1.50 | Yes | No | Yes | Yes |

THE MONTHS, DAYS AND TIMES OF OPERATION WERE CONFIRMED PRIOR TO PUBLICATION OF THIS BOOK. THE AUTHOR IS NOT RESPONSIBLE IF CHANGES ARE MADE TO THESE SCHEDULES.
IT IS ADVISABLE TO CONFIRM THE SCHEDULE PRIOR TO SETTING OUT ON YOUR DAYS TOUR.

# • GARDEN PARTICULARS •

| | GARDEN NAME | CITY | PHONE NUMBER | NATIONAL TRUST | MONTHS OPEN | DAYS OPEN | HOURS OPEN | FEE/ AMOUNT | FOOD SERVICE | PICNIC AREA | REST ROOM | GIFT SHOP |
|---|---|---|---|---|---|---|---|---|---|---|---|---|
| 21 | Heale Garden | Salisbury | 0722 73504 | No | All | Daily | 10:00-5:00 | £2.75. | No | Yes | Yes | Yes |
| 22 | Hever Castle | Edenbridge | 01732 865224 | No | Mar thru Nov | Daily | 11:00-6:00 | £6.50,chd£3.30 | Yes | Yes | Yes | Yes |
| *23 | High Beeches Gardens | Handcross | 01444 400589 | No | Apr-Jun, Sep-Oct | Daily ex Wed | 1:00-5:00 | £3.00, chd free | No | No | Yes | No |
| 24 | Hiller, Sir Harold, Gardens | Romsey | 01794 368787 | No | All | Daily | 10:30-6:00 | £4.00,chd£1.00 | Yes | Yes | Yes | Yes |
| 25 | Hinton Ampner | Bramdean | (0962) 771305 | Yes | Apr thru Sep | Sat,Sun,Tue,Wed,Bk Hol Mon | 1:30-5:30 | £3.90 | Yes | No | Yes | No |
| 26 | Ilford Manor | Bradford on Avon | 01225 863146 | No | May-Sep / Apr & Oct | Daily exMon&Fri / Sun | 2:00-5:00 / 2:00-5:00 | £2.20,chd£1.60 | Yes,wknds | No | Yes | No |
| 27 | Ightham Mote | Sevenoaks | (01732) 810378 | Yes | Apr thru Oct | Daily ex Tue&Sat / Sun,Bk Hol Mon | 12:00-5:30 / 11:00-5:30 | £4.00,chd£2.00 | Yes | Yes | Yes | Yes |
| 28 | Knoll Gardens | Hampreston | 01202 873931 | No | Apr thru Sep | Daily | 10:00-5:00 | £3.25,chd£1.70 | Yes | No | Yes | Yes |
| *29 | Leeds Castle | Maidstone | 01622 765400 | No | Mar thru Oct | Daily | 10:00-5:00 | £6.00,chd£3.70 | Yes | No | Yes | Yes |
| 30 | Leonardslee Gardens | Horsham | 01403 891212 | No | Apr thru Oct | Daily | 10:00-6:00 | £4.50,chd£2.00 | Yes | No | No | Yes |
| 31 | Marle Place | Brenchley | 0189272 2304 | No | Apr thru Oct | Daily | 9:00-5:30 | | Yes | Yes | No | Yes |
| 32 | Merriments Gardens | Hawkhurst | 01580 860666 | No | Apr -Sep | Daily | 10:00-5:00 | £1.50 | No | No | Yes | No |
| 33 | Mompesson House | Salisbury | (01722) 335659 | Yes | April thru Oct | Daily ex Thur & Fri | 12:00-5:30 | £3.20,chd£1.60 | Yes | No | Yes | No |
| 34 | Mottisfont Abbey Garden | Mottisfont | (01794) 340757 | Yes | Apr thru Oct | Sat-Wed | 12:00-6:00 | £4.00,chd£2.00 | Yes | No | Yes | Yes |
| 35 | Nymans Garden | Haywards Heath | (0444) 400321 | Yes | Mar thru Oct | Daily exMon & Tue, Bk Hol Mon | 11:00-7:00 | £4.20,chd£2.10 | Yes | Yes | Yes | Yes |
| 36 | Pashley Manor Gardens | Ticehurst | 01580 200692 | No | Apr thru Sep | Tue,Wed,Thu,Sat,Bk Hol Mon | 11:00-5:00 | £3.50,chd£3.00 | Yes | Yes | Yes | Yes |
| 37 | Penshurst Place | Tunbridge | 01892 870307 | No | Apr-Oct | Daily | 11:00-6:00 | £5.50,chd£3.00 | Yes | Yes | Yes | Yes |
| 38 | Pines, The | St. Margaret | | No | All | Daily | 10:00-5:00 | £1.25,chd35p | Yes | No | Yes | Yes |
| 39 | Polesden Lacey | Dorking | (01372) 452048 | Yes | All | Daily | 11:00-6:00 | £3.00 | Yes | Yes | Yes | Yes |

THE MONTHS, DAYS AND TIMES OF OPERATION WERE CONFIRMED PRIOR TO PUBLICATION OF THIS BOOK. THE AUTHOR IS NOT RESPONSIBLE IF CHANGES ARE MADE TO THESE SCHEDULES.
IT IS ADVISABLE TO CONFIRM THE SCHEDULE PRIOR TO SETTING OUT ON YOUR DAYS TOUR.

# • GARDEN PARTICULARS •

| | GARDEN NAME | CITY | PHONE NUMBER | NATIONAL TRUST | MONTHS OPEN | DAYS OPEN | HOURS OPEN | FEE/ AMOUNT | FOOD SERVICE | PICNIC AREA | REST ROOM | GIFT SHOP |
|---|---|---|---|---|---|---|---|---|---|---|---|---|
| 40 | Scotney Castle | Tunbridge Wells | (0892) 890651 | Yes | Apr thru Oct | Wed-Fri Sat,Sun,Bk Hol | 11:00-6:00 2:00-6:00 | £3.60,chd£1.80 | No | Yes | Yes | Yes |
| *41 | Sheffield Park Garden | Uckfield | (01825) 790231 | Yes | Apr-midNov | Tues-Sun, Bk Hol Mon | 11:00-6:00 | £4.00,chd£2.00 | Yes | Yes | Yes | Yes |
| 42 | Sissinghurst Garden timed tickets during peak hrs | Cranbrook | (0:580) 715330 | Yes | Apr-midOct | Tue-Fri Sat,Su | 1:00-6:30 10:00-5:30 | £6.00,chd£3.00 | Yes | Yes | Yes | Yes |
| 43 | Snape Cottage bed & breakfast also | Bourton | 01747 840330 | No | May thru Jul Apr & Sep | Sun & Wed Wed | 2:00-5:00 2:00-5:00 | £1.50 £1.50 | No | No | No | Yes |
| 44 | Spinners | Lymington | (01590) 673347 | No | mid Apr-midSep | Daily exSun & Mon | 10:00-5:00 | £1.50,chd und 6 fr | No | No | No | Yes |
| 45 | Squerryes Court | Westerham | 01959 562345 | No | Apr-Oct | Wed,Sat,Sun,Bk Hol Mon | 12:00-5:30 | £3.70,chd£1.90 | Yes | Yes | Yes | Yes |
| *46 | Standen | East Grinstead | (0342) 323029 | Yes | Apr thru Oct | Wed-Sun, Bk Hol Mon | 12:30-6:00 | £4.50,chd£2.25 | Yes | No | Yes | Yes |
| 47 | Stourhead | Stourton | (01747) 840348 | Yes | All | Daily | 8:00-7:00 | £4.30,chd£2.30 | No | Yes | Yes | No |
| 48 | Stourton House | Stourton | 01747 840417 | No | Apr thru Nov | Sun,Wed,Th,Bk Hol.Mon | 11:00-6:00 | £2.00,chd50p | Yes | Yes | Yes | Yes |
| 49 | Uppark | Petersfield | (01730) 825857 | Yes | Apr thru Oct | Daily | 12:00-5:30 | £5.00 | Yes | Yes | Yes | Yes |
| 50 | Wakehurst Place Garden | Haywards Heath | (01444) 894066 | No | All | Daily | 10:00-4:00 | £4.00 | Yes | No | Yes | Yes |
| 51 | Walmer Castle | Walmer | 01304 364288 | No | Apr thru Oct | Daily | 10:00-6:00 | £4.00,chd£2.00 | Yes | No | Yes | No |
| 52 | West Dean Gardens | West Dean | 01243 811303 | No | All | Daily | 11:00-5:00 | £3.50,chd£1.50 | Yes | No | Yes | Yes |
| 53 | Gilbert White's House & Garden | Selborne | 01420 511275 | No | Apr-Dec | Daily | 11:00-5:00 | £3.00,chd£1.00 | Yes | No | | |
| 54 | Wilton House | Salisbury | 01722 734115 | No | Apr-Nov | Daily | 11:00-6:00 | £6.20,chd£4.00 | Yes | No | Yes | Yes |
| 55 | Wisley Garden | Woking | 01483 224234 | No | All | Mon-Sat | 10:00-7:00 | £4.90,chd£1.75 | Yes | No | Yes | Yes |

THE MONTHS, DAYS AND TIMES OF OPERATION WERE CONFIRMED PRIOR TO PUBLICATION OF THIS BOOK. THE AUTHOR IS NOT RESPONSIBLE IF CHANGES ARE MADE TO THESE SCHEDULES.
IT IS ADVISABLE TO CONFIRM THE SCHEDULE PRIOR TO SETTING OUT ON YOUR DAY'S TOUR.

# • LIST OF PUBLICATIONS •

**Garden Books**

"Yellow Book", Gardens of England and Wales, for a copy send $18.00 to: The National Gardens Scheme, Hatchlands Park, East Clandon, Guildford, Surrey, GU4 7RT

Garden Style by Penelope Hobhouse; Little, Brown & Company, 1988

A Book of Gardening- The National Trust by Penelope Hobhouse; Little, Brown & Company, 1986

Flower Gardens by Penelope Hobhouse, Little, Brown & Co., 1991

The Ordnance Survey Guide to Gardens in England; W.W. Norton & Company, 1986

The Country House Garden by Gervase Jackson-Stops; Pavilion Books Limited, 1987

The Garden Makers by George Plumptre; Random House, 1993

One Hundred English Gardens by Patrick Taylor; Rizzoli International Publications, Inc, 1996

The National Trust Gardens Handbook, for a copy contact: The National Trust, 36 Queen Anne's Gate, London SW1H 9AS or phone 0171 222 9251

Gardens of the National Trust by Graham Thomas, The National Trust/Weidenfeld & Nicolson, London, 1979

Gardens of England, Scotland & Wales By Hazel Evens, George Philip Limited, 1991

The History of Gardens by Christopher Thacker, University of California Press, 1979

The Art of Planting by Rosemary Verey; Little, Brown & Co., 1990

The Gardens of England, The Counties of Kent, Surrey and Sussex by Rob Talbot & Robin Whiteman; Weidenfeld and Nicolson, London, 1995

The Formal Garden by Mark Laird; Thames and Hudson, London, 1992

## Hotels and B & B's

Bed and Breakfast for Garden Lovers, for a copy send a self addressed envelope with 3 international reply-paid coupons to: BBGL, Handywater Farm, Sibford Gower, Banbury, Oxfordshire OX15 5AE

Cotswold Retreats, for a copy call: Paula at 01608 737222 or Sue at 01608 684310 or fax 01608 684310

The National Trust Bed and Breakfast, for a copy contact: The National Trust, 36 Queen Anne's Gate, London SW1H 9AS or phone 0171 222 9251

England, Charming Bed & Breakfasts; Karen Brown; Travel Press, 1996 or phone (415) 342-9117

England, Wales & Scotland, Charming Hotels & Itineraries; Karen Brown; Travel Press, 1996 or phone (415) 342-9117

# Index

■■■■■■■■■■■■■■■■■■■■■■■■■■■■■■■■■■■■■■■■■■■■

■■■■■■■■■■■■■■■■■■■■■■■■■■■■■■■■■■■■■■■■■■■■

# • ORDER FORM •

- Fax Orders: (510) 934-8002 (send this form)
- On-Line orders: Bonnie Randall-- ukgarden@lanminds.com
- Postal Orders: Windsor Hill Publishing,
  119 Poppy Court, Walnut Creek, Ca. 94596, U.S.A.
- Telephone orders: (510) 934-7761

Please send _____ copies of Garden Tours of England -The Cotswolds

and/or _____copies of Garden Tours of England-The Southern Region

Price $14.95 per copy

Sales tax for those books shipped in California is 8.25%.

Shipping: Book rate is $2.00 for the first book and 75 cents for each additional book (shipping may take 3 to 4 weeks). Air Mail is $3.50 per book.

Please Print:

Name:_____

Address:_____

City:_____State_____Zip:_____

Telephone:_____

|  |  | Total |
|---|---|---|
| Tour Books | _____x $14.95 |  |
| Tax | 8.25% in Calif. |  |
| Shipping |  |  |
| Total |  |  |

Payment:
□ Check

□ Credit Card: □ VISA, □ MasterCard

Card number:_____Exp Date:_____

Name on card:_____

Signature:_____

# • ORDER FORM •

- Fax Orders: (510) 934-8002 (send this form)
- On-Line orders: Bonnie Randall-- ukgarden@lanminds.com
- Postal Orders: Windsor Hill Publishing,
  119 Poppy Court, Walnut Creek, Ca. 94596, U.S.A.
- Telephone orders: (510) 934-7761

Please send _____ copies of Garden Tours of England -The Cotswolds

and/or _____copies of Garden Tours of England-The Southern Region

Price $14.95 per copy

Sales tax for those books shipped in California is 8.25%.

Shipping: Book rate is $2.00 for the first book and 75 cents for each additional book (shipping may take 3 to 4 weeks). Air Mail is $3.50 per book.

Please Print:

Name:_____

Address:_____

City:_____State_____Zip:_____

Telephone:_____

|  |  | Total |
|---|---|---|
| Tour Books | _____x $14.95 |  |
| Tax | 8.25% in Calif. |  |
| Shipping |  |  |
| Total |  |  |

Payment:
▫ Check

▫ Credit Card: ▫ VISA, ▫ MasterCard

Card number:_____Exp Date:_____

Name on card:_____

Signature:_____